workplace skills for students & graduates

How to hit the ground running from your first day on the job

Bill Kirton

Prentice Hall
is an imprint of

Harlow, England • London • New York • Boston • San Francisco • Toronto
Sydney • Tokyo • Singapore • Hong Kong • Seoul • Taipei • New Delhi
Cape Town • Madrid • Mexico City • Amsterdam • Munich • Paris • Milan

PEARSON EDUCATION LIMITED

Edinburgh Gate
Harlow CM20 2JE
Tel: +44 (0)1279 623623
Fax: +44 (0)1279 431059
Website: www.pearson.com/uk

First published in Great Britain in 2012

Pearson Education is not responsible for the content of third-party internet sites.

ISBN: 978-0-273-75704-7

British Library Cataloguing-in-Publication Data
A catalogue record for this book is available from the British Library

Library of Congress Cataloging-in-Publication Data
Kirton, Bill.
  Brilliant workplace skills for students and graduates / Bill Kirton. -- 1st ed.
     p. cm.
  ISBN 978-0-273-75704-7 (pbk.)
1. Career education. 2. Self-confidence. 3. Interpersonal communication. 4. Organizational behavior. I. Title.

  LC1037.K57 2011
  370.113--dc23

                            2011033605

10 9 8 7 6 5 4 3 2 1
15 14 13 12 11

Typeset in 10/14pt Plantin by 30
Printed and bound in Great Britain by Henry Ling Ltd, at the Dorset Press, Dorchester, Dorset

To the memory of my mum and dad, who knew what work was

Contents

About the author

Before taking early retirement to become a full-time writer, **Bill Kirton** was a lecturer in French at the University of Aberdeen. He has also been a Royal Literary Fund Writing Fellow at the RGU in Aberdeen, and the universities of Dundee and St Andrews. His radio plays have been broadcast by the BBC and on the Australian BC. His novels have been published in the UK and USA and his short stories have appeared in several anthologies. He lives in Aberdeen with his wife Carolyn.

His website is www.bill-kirton.co.uk and his blog can be found at http://livingwritingandotherstuff.blogspot.com/

Acknowledgements

Brilliant Workplace Skills for Students & Graduates draws on the research and writings of Ciara Woods as published in *Everything You Need to Know at Work*.

We are grateful to the following for permission to reproduce copyright material:

Figure 4.1 from *Everything You Need to Know at Work*, Prentice Hall (Woods, C. 2003) p. 51; Figure 9.1 from *Everything You Need to Know at Work*, Prentice Hall (Woods, C. 2003) Figure 7.1, p. 80; Figure 9.2 from *Everything You Need to Know at Work*, Prentice Hall (Woods, C. 2003) Figure 7.2, p. 86; Figure 11.1 from *Everything You Need to Know at Work*, Prentice Hall (Woods, C. 2003) Figure 8.1, p. 104

In some instances we have been unable to trace the owners of copyright material, and we would appreciate any information that would enable us to do so.

Introduction: a brave new world

In case you didn't know, the words we've used for the title of this introduction are from Shakespeare's *The Tempest*. Miranda, Prospero's daughter, has led a sheltered life and when she sees people other than her father for the first time, she says:

> How beauteous mankind is! O brave new world,
> That has such people in't!

Well, unless you're very lucky, starting out in the workplace may not set you thinking of mankind as 'beauteous', but it's quite likely to be a 'brave new world'. It's the place we spend a big chunk of most days and, when we add it all up, a lot of our lives. It can be challenging or comfortable, frustrating or exhilarating, dull or exciting and many combinations of all of these and more. The aim of this book is to identify in advance some of the experiences you may have, help you negotiate both the ups and downs of life at work and make it a place of enjoyment as well as fulfilment.

The word 'workplace' could refer to anything from the international space station to the driver's seat in a taxi so here, for the sake of convenience and ease of comprehension, we mostly call it the office. But the points we make apply to any situation in which you're working with other people within a structured hierarchy which has bosses, teams, departments or other groupings. In the end, almost everything connected with work comes down to interacting with people – either directly, face to face, or through procedures, processes and systems which they've created.

Another point to make about our treatment of the subject is the style we've chosen. It's deliberately conversational. So, if your job involves writing reports or any other sort of 'official' documents, don't use this as a model. We say 'It's', 'don't', 'we'll' and use all the other contractions normally only found in speech. We also make grammatical 'errors'. For example, one sentence reads: 'you'll have a better idea of who to cultivate and who to avoid' which, of course, in 'correct' English should end 'whom to cultivate and whom to avoid'. But this is deliberate and we're choosing to use this approach not from any lack of respect for the rules of grammar and stylistic 'purity' but because we think an informal approach is easier to read.

A final point about style – gender equality is an important issue and it can raise problems in any written text. To respect the equality of women and men, people write sentences such as: 'If your boss is difficult to talk to, you must let him or her know that he or she is only making life difficult for himself or herself'. That's obviously an ugly, clumsy construction which actually interferes with the reading process. To work round it, we've decided to use he, she, him, her at random throughout, so sometimes a colleague, client or boss is male, sometimes female.

The book's divided into three main sections, the first of which deals with the basics of getting to know people, equipment and procedures. After that, we focus on the sort of skills you need to develop to cope with problems, conduct research, handle financial matters and give presentations. Then we move to the whole business of working with people in teams, managing your boss, your clients and yourself, negotiating issues relating to office politics and maintaining a comfortable balance between work and your private life.

Work is sometimes seen as a necessary evil. As J. M. Barrie wrote: 'Nothing is really work unless you would rather be doing something else'. If that's the way you approach it, with a negative perception of what to expect, you may find it's a self-fulfilling prophesy. It's just as legitimate to see it as a game, with rules, tactics, winners, losers, satisfactions and rewards. Remember, in all games, positive attitudes are the keys to success.

PART 1

The groundwork

CHAPTER 1

First
impressions

U nless you have a job as a hermit, your work will involve interacting with others. There'll be colleagues of course, but maybe also members of the public, suppliers, business partners, government officials, and more. It'll obviously make life easier for everyone involved, including you, if you get on well with them rather than alienating them in some way. This chapter considers some of the basics of social interaction in the workplace, suggesting who you need and don't need to know, how to handle small talk, remember names, be a good listener and communicate well both face to face and on the phone.

Thin-slicing

A footballer receives the ball and, almost instantaneously, passes it to the feet of someone else on his team. The speed of thought is bewildering. This, and other examples of sportspeople behaving almost instinctively as they shoot for the hoop, drive a forehand across court, slam a baseball or cricket ball into a gap between fielders – they're all the result of what psychologists call 'thin-slicing'. In other words, people make fast decisions and perform actions on the basis of split-second observations of thin slices of information.

But it's not just sportsmen and sportswomen who do it. Apparently that's what we all do most of the time and, surprisingly perhaps, we're usually right. So what's it got to do with workplace skills? Well, the suggestion is that that's how we form impressions of others. We meet them, form an opinion of them within the first few seconds and, from then on, just notice things which confirm that impression.

This may come as an unpleasant surprise if you've spent ages preparing for an interview or working out how to impress the future in-laws, because it suggests that the first handshake, eye contact, hairstyle choice, colour of jacket or goodness knows what else has already made up the mind of the person you're meeting before you've uttered a word. On the other hand, if you're aware of how this process works, you can focus on those first impressions and make sure you use them to your advantage.

Need to know or need to avoid

There isn't a handy 'people check list' we can offer you because each workplace will have different dynamics and procedures, but we can generalise about the sort of people you should try to get to know and those you should avoid. You'll obviously need to meet those in your peer group, your boss, her boss, people in other departments and in human resources. Once you get settled, you'll have a better idea of who to cultivate and who to avoid. But don't think of every encounter as a transaction. Be natural, open and develop positive contacts with like-minded colleagues. It won't just make the job easier; it'll also make day-to-day life more pleasant.

brilliant tip

Workplaces develop hierarchies which are sometimes signalled by expressions such as 'upper', 'middle' or 'lower management'. There obviously has to be such a structure and some people do wield more power than others, but don't underestimate the importance of the support services, secretaries or personal assistants.

Choose with care

Mentors are a great help both when you're starting out and as you settle in and need more detailed information. Some companies assign one to you as part of their policy. This is fine but the relationship with them doesn't always work out as well as it should, so there's no harm in trying to persuade someone you get on with (preferably someone with influence) to be an informal mentor. And beware of anyone who tells you things 'in confidence', especially if it's something they're supposed to be keeping secret. You need to be with people you can trust.

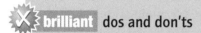 **dos and don'ts**

Do cultivate

✔ People who make things happen

✔ People who give you advice, support and feedback

✔ People who provide access to information

✔ People who can introduce you to others

✔ People who've shown they're willing to help you

Don't waste time with ...

✘ People who talk too much

✘ People on the same level as you who are overly competitive

✘ People who have negative attitudes about work-related things

✘ People who depress you or create stress for those around them

First contacts

Ideally, whoever you're meeting, the impression you want to create is that you're professional, confident and likeable. This may sound cynical and false, but making and developing contacts within your own organisation and others is a positive, necessary skill to acquire. Whatever your opinion of your own worth, success will depend on working with others and being aware of what's going on in your particular field and industry. Meeting and getting to know new people, expanding your circle of acquaintances and making new friendships will all help you to learn more about the business you're in and establish you as part of it.

Don't hold back

If there's someone you'd like to meet or you think might help you in some way, don't just wait for it to happen; find a way of getting to know them. Send them an email, call them on the phone or get someone to introduce you. Find out the sort of things they like and whether you have any common interests. And don't just concentrate on what they might do for you; think about what you could offer them. It sounds transactional but that's true of so many social contacts that it's a normal way of interacting.

Keep in touch

Once you've made contact, make sure you maintain it. Make a note of their names and addresses and any other useful information. Invite them to special events or social occasions, send them things you read in the papers or journals that you think they'll be interested in, and don't forget to congratulate them on domestic or other events, such as engagements, marriages, new babies or, of course, promotions at work.

If you make a promise, make sure you keep it. If someone asks you to do something for them, do it quickly, with no strings attached, and show them they can trust you. Giving is as important as taking. Be sincere. If you're always on the make, you'll soon become one of the people others are trying to avoid.

In the end, it boils down to showing mutual respect. Be ready to make your own judgements but recognise the value of the opinions of others.

brilliant tip

When you start work, you'll probably get to meet senior people who won't be so accessible later on as you settle into your place in the organisation. This is a good chance to begin to establish yourself, so don't be afraid to say something. There's no need to give them a stand-up routine or be pushy or over-enthusiastic, but a simple, confident 'hello' will create a positive impression. It's that vital 'thin-slice'.

Introductions

Remember the importance of first impressions. When you're meeting people for the first time, always stand up or move towards them as they approach (even if they've said 'Don't get up'). Make and keep eye contact, smile, offer your hand for them to shake and tell them your first and last name in a clear, friendly tone. If it's one of your peers or the setting's informal, you can just give your first name.

Be ready for any questions they might ask by having in your mind a sort of brief summary about yourself – where you're from, your university or previous job, your role in the company, the people you'll be working with. Keep it all open, friendly and interesting.

brilliant tip

Don't underestimate the importance of the handshake. There's a happy medium between the limp offering that makes them feel they're holding a damp rag and the bone-crunching, macho power-play. Just squeeze their hand firmly and shake it two or three times from the elbow not the wrist. It should be a calm, reassuring gesture, not a frenzied sort of arm-dance.

In a group

If there are several people starting with a company at the same time, introductions may be made in a group. Frequently this means you all sit in a big circle and introduce yourselves to the rest one by one. In some ways, this is harder than the individual introduction because it's a sort of performance. You feel you've got to interest or amuse the audience as well as tell them who you are, so you should give it plenty of thought beforehand because it's an experience that may be repeated at training courses or meetings.

The people who organise these meetings or courses often try to make the introductions more interesting by asking you questions about yourself. Some common ones are:

- Do you have an interesting fact or story to tell us about yourself?
- What's the most embarrassing thing that's happened to you?
- Which five words best describe you?
- What are your hobbies?
- If you weren't doing this job, what would you do?

You can no doubt add more of the same. They're all things you can prepare (or invent) to project a favourable image of yourself.

Remembering names

For most of us, seeing a person and trying desperately to remember his name is a familiar experience. In a way, forgetting his name can seem like an insult to him, perhaps suggesting he's not important to you. And, if you do remember, it has the reverse effect, making him feel important and valued. So try to develop a technique for remembering names when you're introduced. At some point, you may also need to introduce them to someone else and it's embarrassing if you find yourself asking 'What's your name again?'

So, listen carefully the first time you hear the name. Focus on it the first time he says it, keeping eye contact with him and repeating it in one of the normal formulas, such as 'Nice to meet you, Richard'. Don't be distracted by other things; make a mental note of it and, if you didn't hear it clearly, apologise and ask him to repeat it.

Try to connect it visually with some aspect of the person, such as the shape of his face, colour of his eyes, his height. Don't choose something that may change, like the style of his glasses, the colour of his jacket or his Homer Simpson tie. This will give you a hook to help fix it in your mind. Try also to use his name as often as you can in the conversation you have with him (without sounding like a parrot), and use it again when you say goodbye. After every meeting with anyone new, write down their names, adding the feature you associate it with too, if you like. Just seeing it written down will help you to remember it.

And if you genuinely can't remember it, ask again as soon as possible. It needn't be embarrassing; lots of people have the same difficulty, but if you are embarrassed, suggest exchanging business cards with him.

brilliant tip

The excuse 'I'm terrible at remembering names' is feeble and won't convey a good impression to the other person, so don't rely on it. And don't accept that it's true. Work at being good at it, try out different techniques to find one that works for you. It's an extremely important skill and you can certainly improve at it.

Small talk

The introduction is important, but it's just the beginning. If it's followed by an awkward silence, that all-important first impression is going to be a negative one. So develop the skill of making small talk. Sometimes, it's not easy, but if you work at it and become proficient, you'll make the other person feel more comfortable and help to project a positive image of yourself. So ...

- **... try to make them feel important**
  Don't assume that what interests you will be equally enthralling for them. However strongly you feel about a topic, you'll be more successful if you find out what interests them and focus on that. It'll make them feel at ease, and it's easier to build a relationship by massaging their ego than by indulging your own. Again, that may sound cynical but it's just realistic. They'll be in their comfort zone – you just need to find what their special interest is. Once you've found it, you won't need to talk as much because they'll take over.

- **... try to find some common ground**
  It's even better if you can find an interest you share. It might be a country you've both been to, an exhibition, movie or play you've both seen, a book you've read. Whatever it is, make sure you focus on the similarities between you rather than the differences.

- **... avoid inappropriate subjects**
  These will vary according to circumstances but you can probably list for yourself the sort of things that you shouldn't discuss when you're with someone, especially a stranger, in a business context.

- **... mean what you say**
  The way we're talking about this may be making it sound like role play, but that's not the intention. OK, it's 'only' small talk, but it's serving a purpose and it helps if you're sincere. If you're not, most people you speak to will sense that and you'll go down in their estimation and seem like a poser. Keep it light, pleasant and interesting, and don't indulge in flattery.

It's better for everyone if this sort of small talk is enjoyable. If you enjoy the time you spend with them, it's more likely they'll feel the same way. But don't get stressed about it; the more you do it, the easier it gets. And remember, they'll usually be far more interested in their own lives than yours.

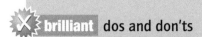 **dos and don'ts**

Do discuss

✔ How you got to the meeting and any interesting things that occurred en route

✔ Cultural or sporting events

✔ Books, films, magazine or newspaper articles

✔ Happy occasions such as weddings or births or upbeat news items

✔ General business events or news

Don't discuss

✘ Their or your marital status (including divorce and any other aspects of marriage that should stay private)

✘ Matters concerning health

✘ Personal finance (including salary)

✘ Things which could be perceived as rude or racist

✘ Religion and politics of any persuasion

And, even though you think a particular joke is killingly funny, remember that they may not share your sense of humour so, at least in the early stages of an acquaintanceship, it's probably wise to avoid jokes altogether.

Be a good listener

If you find yourself in a conversation where the other person is doing most of the talking, you're doing a good job. You don't want to seem shy, reticent or submissive, but listening attentively and responding with a relevant remark at the right time is a great skill and will earn you at least as much approval as if you were a brilliant conversationalist. It shows you're interested in the other person and what they're saying and that you have the self-confidence to let them have the floor.

It's not just a passive skill. Once you've found a topic they're interested in, encourage them to speak and make sure they take up at least half of the conversation. If they look as if they need encouragement, ask their opinion with open-ended questions.

 **definition**

Open-ended question

One which typically begins with words such as 'Why', 'How', or phrases such as 'Tell me about...'. Its aim is to produce a full answer based on the personal knowledge and/or feelings of the person being asked.

Closed-ended question

One which encourages a short or single-word answer.

Concentrate on what's being said

Give the person speaking your undivided attention. Don't let things such as her appearance or accent distract you; ignore wasps, flies or other nuisances, and resist the temptation to eavesdrop on a nearby conversation. Don't try working out a response as you're listening, and don't interrupt her unless you want to ask a question or make sure you've understood what she's said. It might be useful to summarise her words when you do this, just to make sure. And if you don't have time to listen, fix a time when you're both free to continue the conversation.

Don't just listen selectively

You should be using more than your ears as you listen. Watch her body language, think about what she's saying, listen for underlying meanings, emotional signals, things that are left unspoken. When she's finished, you should be able to list for yourself all the key points she made.

Keep an open mind

You may start forming opinions about the person who's speaking or you may already have preconceptions about him. Don't let that get in the way of how you interpret what he says, and never assume you know what he's going to say or that he means something different from what his words suggest. You should be looking for points on which you agree rather than differences. Don't start silently arguing with him in your head and don't get emotive or defensive.

Don't just pretend to listen; let the person see that you're hearing what he's saying by maintaining eye contact with him and making supportive comments and gestures. And, whatever you see out of the corner of your eye, resist the temptation to look past him at it. That's very rude and you can be sure he'll notice it.

In the end, it comes down to empathy. If you try to see things from his point of view, it'll be easier to get on.

 **brilliant** recap

- The importance of creating a positive first impression.
- How to identify and deal with people you want to contact and those you want to avoid.
- Introducing yourself to individuals and in groups.
- Tips on how to remember names.
- The importance of small talk and some strategies on how to become proficient at using it.

CHAPTER 2

Talking with confidence

A s we've seen, being a good listener is important but, of course, you need to be a good talker, too. You need to interest others enough to make them want to talk with you. In the end, it comes down to confidence, but there are strategies you can use to help build that confidence, and the more you make yourself take the initiative, the easier it all becomes. In this chapter we'll shift the focus to concentrate on speaking face to face and on the phone.

Self-control and self-projection

We're still focusing on the impression you create as you interact with others. You want to show that you believe in what you're saying, and that you're confident about it. Try to keep it brief and to the point but don't just make it a series of bullet points – liven it up with examples, quotes, humour and anecdotes. Vary your tone and avoid the tendency to let your voice lift at the end of each sentence. That makes it sound as if you're uncertain and asking questions all the time.

Once again, eye contact is important. If you let your gaze flick about or wander, it can make you look evasive. That doesn't mean you have to stare, but keeping that personal contact gives what you're saying more impact.

Choosing your conversations

It's natural for all of us to want to speak to some people but avoid speaking to others for all sorts of reasons. The important thing is that you mustn't let your likes or dislikes show either way. So if it's someone you want to speak to, don't rush up to him and seem too eager to be in his company. Wait until you see he's alone or can be approached without disturbing him unduly. If others try to talk to you while you're on your way to him, be polite to them but don't let them start up a conversation.

If you want to avoid someone, the simplest way is not to approach or encourage them. But they may still approach you so, if they do, be polite, greet them but don't let the small talk get going. Excuse yourself, tell them there's something you have to deal with, smile and move away or return to the task that needs your urgent attention.

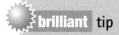 **tip**

It's usually much more productive to make a few meaningful, memorable contacts than to flit around chatting with lots of people.

Rudeness and reactions

Being rude is never justified. Even when the person you're trying to avoid is annoyingly persistent, be polite. And, if others are rude to you when you try to make conversation, don't sink to their level. If you're snubbed in that way, stay calm and try turning the remark they made back on themselves. Don't let them see that it's affected you but let them know it was rude by asking them, calmly and politely, to explain what they meant. They'll probably end up digging a deeper hole for themselves.

We can all think of the witty thing we should have said in reply to a snub, but by the time we do it's usually too late, so just forget about it and move on. Don't give them the satisfaction of showing that it offended you and don't start a sort of playground contest to show which of you is better at ignoring the other.

Just be yourself and stay in control. If you let their remarks get to you, you're letting them dictate what happens. No one can make you feel inferior unless you let them. So make it clear that you're not going to react to whatever it is they've said. And if they ask you questions or continue with the rudeness, don't respond. If a question isn't answered, it's usually more uncomfortable and embarrassing for the person who asked it than for yourself.

brilliant dos and don'ts

Do

✔ Express your ideas and opinions with confidence and conviction

✔ Control and vary the way you speak

✔ Project your voice when you're speaking to a group

✔ Speak clearly and correctly

Don't

✘ Express self-doubt or seem to be making excuses

✘ Mumble

✘ Laugh nervously or give other signs of embarrassment or lack of confidence

✘ Use slang, nicknames or swear words

Conversational strategies

It's natural enough to be a bit defensive at the beginning of a conversation with someone you've just met. Neither of you is ready to drop his guard until he knows he can trust the other. So try to find common ground so that you can enter each other's world. It can be a bit tricky because, if the other person thinks you're just barging into his private territory, his defences will be even higher.

Make it as relaxed as possible. Talk to him respectfully, listen and let him know somehow that you're not trying to compete with him. Don't boast or show off in any way and, if you do try asking more personal questions, wrap them up a bit in expressions such as 'Do you mind if I ask you ...?'

brilliant tip

If you're keen to get on to a specific topic, don't force it; approach it gently, hesitating a bit and just suggesting it as a possibility. You'll quickly learn whether it's OK or not, either by him saying he'd rather not talk about it or through his body language. If he nods and leans forward it suggests he's interested, but if he folds his arms and avoids making eye contact, it's probably better to change the subject.

Body language

All the gestures we make and the stances we take up are part of the whole communication process. If you can read these non-verbal messages, you'll learn even more than by just listening. People can be careful with their words, but their bodies sometimes give them away. If you learn a bit about body language, your own and other people's, it'll give you more control. Think about your personal habits and the typical gestures you make and practise controlling them so that you can make sure you're sending out the right signals.

Of course, body language isn't as easy to understand as the spoken word. It depends on where you are, what your own personal habits are, and the context in which you find yourself. There's no dictionary that tells you a specific sign always means the same thing. We mentioned folded arms because that's usually thought to be a defensive gesture, but it might just be because the person feels cold. It's a question of being observant and aware of changes of expression or tone.

brilliant dos and don'ts

Do

- ✔ Sit or stand up straight
- ✔ Keep your body facing towards the person you're speaking to
- ✔ Hold your head high
- ✔ Relax your arms and legs
- ✔ Smile
- ✔ Make eye contact (although in some cultures this isn't appropriate)
- ✔ Respect people's personal space

Don't

- ✘ Tower over someone
- ✘ Hunch your shoulders when you stand
- ✘ Slouch when you sit
- ✘ Stare at the floor
- ✘ Fold your arms or cross your legs
- ✘ Scratch your head
- ✘ Fidget with your hair, pen, notes or anything else

On the phone

When you're phoning someone or taking a call, body language isn't a factor. But it can pose its own problems, especially if the call's important, you don't know the other person, or if you're in an open plan office.

Making calls

Before you start, think about why you're calling, who the best person to speak to is and what you want to say. Make sure you're calling at an appropriate time too, especially if it's an international call. If you need to refer to notes or other materials, make sure they're at hand. When the person answers, tell them, as briefly as possible, the purpose of the call. Don't waffle or sprinkle your sentences with 'um' and 'er'.

Don't gallop through your words – speak clearly and give your name and company or department if necessary. If you have questions to ask, keep them clear and simple and give the other person time to answer. Spell any difficult names and repeat contact numbers.

If you have a loud voice, try to keep it at a level that's loud enough for you to be heard clearly, but quiet enough not to disturb others around you, especially if you're in an open plan office. If it's a real problem, try to find an empty office from which to make the call.

Be friendly and courteous to everyone, including switchboard operators, secretaries and anyone who's simply connecting you to the person you want to speak with. Check that it's a convenient time to call. If they say it has to be quick, tell them honestly how long you think it'll take.

Take as much care ending a call as you did starting and continuing it. Don't suddenly ring off but, if you're finding it difficult to get away, explain that you have to go to a meeting and thank them for their time.

brilliant tip

It's best to avoid making personal calls in the office. If you have to, though, be discreet and brief and make sure you're not disturbing anyone.

Taking calls

Don't let a phone ring more than three times before answering and, when you pick it up, have a professional greeting ready – not just 'Hi' or 'Hello' but something like 'Good morning/ afternoon. Sheila McCall speaking'. 'My name is Sheila McCall' sounds like the beginning of a confession, whereas 'This is Sheila McCall' is neutral and inoffensive. If you need to, you can also give the name of your company or department, but don't turn it into a grand list of things.

Be careful with your tone of voice. If you've been interrupted by the call or it's inconvenient, it's too easy to let your irritation show and it'll be noticed. Stay polite and always try to be helpful. If the call's about something you can deal with, do so. Don't pass it on to someone else.

If you're not ready to take the call or you don't have the information you need for it, don't waste the caller's time. Ask if you can call her back later. If you do take the call, make sure that you both agree on any decisions that have been made and end it with a quick summary of those decisions and what each of you needs to do about them and by when it must be done.

Always make sure, before you end the call, that you know the caller's name and contact details, and let her hang up first.

All these suggestions amount to common sense and basic politeness, but you shouldn't underestimate their importance. Answering calls properly, leaving clear messages, staying friendly, polite and communicative – they're all indications that you have a professional attitude and approach. You want to create a positive impression and you won't achieve that if you're stumbling, incoherent or rambling. And, even if your caller is rude or aggressive, don't play his game. Stay in control.

brilliant tip

Email can be helpful, especially when you're planning to discuss something over the phone. Send an email to the person you'll be calling and give her time to read and absorb it before you get in touch. You can also send another afterwards to make sure you both agree on who's doing what by when.

Taking a call for someone else

If you have to answer someone else's phone, make it clear right away that you're not the person the caller is looking for by saying something like: 'Hello, Jack Deacon's line. Tony Carr speaking'.

Tell them why 'Jack' isn't available before you ask their name. If you don't they may think he's just avoiding them. As you say why he's unavailable, don't give out any personal information, such as 'He's gone to the doctor's' or 'He's not in yet'. Keep everything positive and professional. If you have to give an excuse, don't make it a vague, feeble one ('He's busy'), and don't use the same one every time ('He's in a meeting'). Also, try to give the caller an idea of when 'Jack' should be available.

You could offer to get him to call them back later. Alternatively you could suggest they stay on the line, but you should give them a realistic idea of how long they might have to wait. Never leave a caller on hold for more than three minutes. Let her know what's happening and ask her if she still wants to hold. Each time you get back to her, remember to thank her for holding.

You could also ask if you, or someone else, can help her in 'Jack's' absence. If you then need to transfer the call, tell her that's what you're going to do. Explain why and tell her who you're transferring her to. Stay with her until the new connection's been made. Tell the person you're transferring her to what she wants so that she doesn't have to repeat it all.

Taking a message

When you take a message, note the date and time, the caller's name and contact details and why they're calling. Check how the name is spelled and get the phone number with the correct area code. It's also worth reading the message back to the caller to make sure it's correct. Put the message in a place where you're confident your colleague will see it and make sure to check later that he did get it.

> ✸ **brilliant** tip
>
> If you might have to transfer calls, learn how to before you receive any. It's usually a straightforward process but if there's any element of pressure it can become stressful.

Voicemail

If the person you're calling isn't there, you may have to leave a message, so plan what you'll say and maybe make a few notes before you call. If you haven't done that and you find that you need to leave a message, ring off, think through what you want to say, then ring back. Don't be tempted to improvise because it may simply produce a long, rambling message which is repetitive and not very clear.

To structure your message:

- Give your name (and company or department, if appropriate).
- If there's no identifying message, say who you're calling.
- If it's the first time you've called them, tell them where you got their name and number.
- Note the time and date.
- Tell them briefly why you're calling and, if it's a complicated message, say you'll email the details to them.

- Tell them what you'll do next, which may be that you'll call back or wait for them to get in touch with you.

- Say how urgent it is, and leave your number, which you should repeat to give them a chance to make a note of it.

This is making it all sound very long-winded and formal, but you should aim to make it as brief and as natural as possible. If it does need to be long and you know you'll need to leave more than one message, say so: 'This is the first of two messages I'm leaving'. If you hadn't anticipated it but you find your message needs to be continued, say so at the end of the first and the beginning of the second – 'The message will be continued on a second voicemail' and 'This a continuation voicemail from Tony about the agenda for the Thursday meeting'.

 **brilliant** tip

What happens sometimes is that people keep calling one another, returning calls, and failing to connect each time. If this happens, tell them you'll call again at a specific time. It's then important that you do so because you won't be popular if the person has kept his line free and the promised call doesn't happen.

Your own voicemail greeting

Even in your absence, you want to create a good impression, so try not to sound bored or mechanical. Make the message brief, cheerful but businesslike. The most frequently used formula is something like 'This is Simon Ross's voicemail. I'm sorry I can't take your call now. Please leave your name, number and a brief message and I'll get back to you'.

If you're not going to be able to listen to your messages for a while, update the message to say so. Tell callers how you can be contacted if it's urgent or suggest someone else who may be able to deal with the issue while you're unavailable. Remember to change the message back when you return.

 **recap**

● How to be good at both listening and talking.

● Some thoughts on body language.

● The techniques of taking and making phone calls.

CHAPTER 3

Technology in the office

The rapid advance of technology has made huge differences to the way we work. We can be more efficient, communicate more easily, access vast amounts of information and shape it in a variety of ways to send it on to others. On the other hand, it's also made us more reliant on support services and, when a system or piece of equipment decides to stop working or seize up, it can be very frustrating. We're not all technicians, but getting a basic understanding of how the different types of technology work does cut down on that frustration and help you to work more efficiently. So here we'll look at the basics of the familiar, everyday technology, see how we can use it more effectively and minimise the stress caused by glitches.

Using it

First, though, let's make sure we use it in a way that doesn't harm us. If your job involves being at a computer for long periods of time, you need to be careful about how you sit and move as you work.

Your position

Adjust your chair so that it's right for your height, makes it easy for you to reach your desk and allows you to sit properly and comfortably. Your legs should be perpendicular to the floor, with both feet flat on the ground and your weight spread evenly. Make sure the small of your back is supported, keep your knees lower than your hips and don't cross your legs.

Sit upright with your elbows level with the keyboard and your wrists relaxed. If you're using the phone, hold it in your hand. Don't try jamming it between your chin and shoulder – you could damage your neck.

The computer screen

Your screen should be at eye level so that you can look at the top of it without straining your neck. Make sure it's directly in front of you at a distance which makes it easy to read. Clean it regularly and, if there's glare on it, get an antiglare cover. Don't sit staring at it for ages; take a five-minute rest from it every hour. Use the time to make a phone call, get a drink, stretch your legs, but give your eyes a rest. You should also have them tested every year.

Deal with discomfort

If you do feel any pain after you've been using your computer for a long period, get yourself checked right away. Make an appointment with a physiotherapist.

Basic technology

In among all the marvellous time-saving devices we use, the telephone is so familiar and has been around so long that we take it for granted and hardly see it as technology. But there are different systems and networks so you'd better make sure you know how yours works. If there's a guide book, get it from Human Resources. If not, ask a colleague to show you.

You'll need to know how to:

● get an outside line, which usually involves dialling 9 or 0;
● call the switchboard;

● make an internal call – this may seem obvious but sometimes there are short dial systems to make it easier;

● forward a call;

● set up and access your voicemail and direct calls to it;

● direct office phone calls to your mobile.

Mobiles

As working conditions have become more flexible, so mobile phones have become more important in the office. Most people have one nowadays. If you don't, you may be given one or encouraged to get one. Just be careful how you use it.

Ring tones

Novelty or comic ring tones always seem like a good idea at the time but they can be very annoying. You don't have to be totally conformist but try to choose one that's civilised and won't irritate the people around you. Jokey ring tones are very unprofessional.

Location and security

Using a mobile can give you a false sense of security and informality, so you may relax your guard when you use them in a way you wouldn't on a normal landline. Be aware of this and never make work-related calls or discuss sensitive work-related issues in public places. When you're at a bus stop or in a café, it may seem a good idea to use the time to get some work done, but there'll be plenty of people around to hear what you're saying.

Juggling calls

If there's an incoming call when you're already on another line, you can either check who's calling, switch your mobile off and call them back later, or ask the person you're speaking to to excuse you, answer the mobile, tell them the situation and say you'll ring them back when you've finished the other call, then go back to the first caller.

 **tip**

Always switch your mobile off during meetings, business lunches and, if you leave it on your desk, any time you'll be elsewhere and unable to answer it.

Conference calls

Meetings happen all the time and it's a nuisance when you can't call one because not everyone's there. That's where conference calls come in. They can bring together people who are in different locations.

Setting up a call

There are specialist companies which organise conference calls. Ask around to find out if your own company uses a regular one. If it doesn't, find one in the *Yellow Pages*.

When you book the call, give them your name, your company and, if you have one, your account number. Also tell them:

- the time and date of the call you want to book;
- how long it'll last;
- how many people will be involved;
- the name of the chairperson.

Some companies will provide a transcript or tape recording of the meeting. If you want this, make sure you choose one which offers the facility.

Make a note of the dial-in number and booking reference they give you and keep these somewhere secure in case you need to make any changes. Send the details of the call – the time, date, dial-in number and chairperson's name – to everyone who'll be taking part and to their PAs and secretaries. If people are dialling in from abroad, make sure they get all the necessary codes. And if, for any reason, you have to cancel the call, do it well before the time for which it was scheduled. If you don't, you'll still be charged for it.

brilliant tip

If the meeting is going to involve discussing presentations, facts and figures, or any other data or information, in whatever form, make sure you send copies out to everyone well in advance so that they can look at them beforehand.

Taking part in a call

● Keep the details of how to connect in a safe place and make sure you can get them when you need them.

● Think about whether you need to book a conference telephone and an office, especially if one or more of the other people involved is going to share it with you.

● Remember that mobiles can interfere with reception when they ring, so switch yours off and, if you're chairing the meeting, remind others to do so.

● When you dial in, say who's chairing the conference and give your name and details as well as those of any other people who are there with you.

● Make a note of the number you have to call or the button you have to press if you get a bad line. And, if the problems continue, ring off and redial.

Videoconferences

All of these suggestions apply equally to videoconferences, which obviously offer visual as well as aural contact, and so bring a 'face-to-face' dimension to the meeting. To set one up, you need to do exactly what we listed for the ordinary conference calls, although they're usually arranged for you in-house by the company's technology services department. The audio link is always two-way but you can choose to have one-way or two-way video.

In most offices, because of the extra technology involved, these conferences tend to be held in particular rooms, so you'll need to reserve the place at least a week in advance.

If you're taking part in one, make sure you arrive early so that you can get to know exactly how it works and what you need to do. And during the conference, try not to move too much – moving images on video are often blurred.

Fax machines

Not so long ago, everyone used faxes, then along came email, which could do more or less the same thing and was quicker and easier to use. But many companies and organisations still do use faxes to send information. If yours is one of them, here are some things to bear in mind when sending a fax.

- Use a pen and write in bold capitals. Pencil messages are harder to read because they don't print clearly.
- On most fax machines, the paper must be fed in with the printed side downwards.
- You may need to dial a number – often it's 9 – to get an external line.
- Make sure you've entered the right number and give it a final check before you press 'Send'.
- It takes ages to send something on dark coloured paper, so avoid it if you can.
- Don't use faxes for invitations, thank you letters or confidential or contentious information.

brilliant tip

Always check the transmission page to confirm that the fax has actually been sent. Just because all the pages have gone through, it doesn't necessarily mean that they've been transmitted.

Photocopiers

In principle, photocopiers are fairly straightforward things but using them can sometimes get stressful. The modern ones are becoming more and more complicated, with lots of options. Some have a security feature so you may need a card or code to use them. You should get to know what they can do and how to get the best results.

These are some of the most common options.

- You can feed in what you need to copy either by putting one sheet at a time on the glass or by putting lots of pages into the automatic feeder on top.
- The paper can be printed either in landscape or portrait format.
- You can use different types of paper – white, coloured or acetate.
- You can make recto verso copies – in other words copy both sides of the page.
- Documents can be made larger or smaller.
- They can also be sorted and stapled.

brilliant tip

Photocopiers always seem to follow Murphy's Law. In other words, if you're in a hurry, they jam. So, if you need to copy something for a meeting, give yourself plenty of time to do it. And if the copier does jam, don't just walk away and leave it for someone else to sort out. You expect it to be working, so does everyone else who uses it.

Printers

You may have access to a laser or an inkjet printer. Laser ones are much more expensive, but they're usually much quicker and give higher quality printouts. Most organisations network their printing, so you probably won't have your own machine but your computer will be connected to a printer that you'll share with other people. So if you've got a large document to print out, try to do it in batches of maybe 10 to 15 pages so that other people can get access to the printer.

Like most of the pieces of equipment we're mentioning, printers can seem temperamental. So, if your pages don't get printed, make sure that:

● your computer's connected to the network;

● the printer's plugged in and hasn't run out of paper or ink;

● your page isn't stuck in a long printing queue. You can check this by clicking on the printer icon.

Scanners

Scanners are basically photocopiers which copy text and/or images into a computer file rather than on to paper. They're useful when you need to add pictures to a presentation or send an article or other document to a colleague electronically. The computer has special dedicated software which lets it interface with the scanner. Once you've copied an image, you can alter it if you need to and then print it out.

Overhead projectors

These are really simple to use and invaluable for meetings and presentations. You just need to prepare some acetates, which are transparent plastic sheets on which you can write, draw or print, then put them on the overhead and they're projected on to a screen behind you. All you have to do is make sure the lens is in focus and the acetate's the right way up.

brilliant tip

If you want to draw attention to a particular feature on an acetate, use a pen and point to it on the acetate rather than reaching up or across to the screen.

There are many other pieces of equipment you may come across but it's not possible to give exhaustive advice here on how to use them all. The best idea is to get to know each machine you need and always leave plenty of time before your meeting or presentation to make sure it's working and deal with any glitches.

Software

The predominance of Microsoft Windows in the marketplace means that most of the software you'll use will have very similar screen layouts and commands.

These are the most common packages:

- **Word** is a word processing programme. The names of the files you use and create in it all end in .doc or .docx to indicate how they're formatted.

- **PowerPoint** is for creating slide shows and other presentations. Its format is .ppt.

- **Excel** is for creating spreadsheets and the format is .xls.

- **Access**, whose format is .mdb, is for building databases.

Software problems

Writing software is a complicated and highly specialised skill and we can't expect programmers to anticipate everything that people may try to do with what they've designed. So you may try pressing a sequence of keys which give commands that the software 'doesn't understand' because they're not part of its program. The result? The program 'doesn't work'. If that happens, we say the software has a 'bug', which can be anything from something mildly annoying to a major computer crash as a result of which you lose all the data you've saved.

Fixing a crash

If your computer does crash, the first thing to do is try to close the particular software you're using. Call up the list of tasks your computer's working on by pressing CTRL, ALT and DEL at the same time. Then highlight the task which is causing the problem and click on 'End task'. The crashed program will shut down and you can go on using the computer, so you can reopen the program and try again.

brilliant tip

If you seem to have lost some files when there's been a crash, don't panic. Quite often, you'll find copies of the 'lost' documents in your temporary files or in the Recycle Bin.

Rebooting

If you need to reboot the computer, press CTRL, ALT, DEL twice or click on the Start menu and choose 'Restart'. If it's frozen completely and isn't responding to any commands, press and hold the on/off switch for several seconds, disconnect the computer from all sources of power, including batteries, leave it off for a minute and then turn it back on.

Technical support

If neither of these procedures solves your problem, you need to contact your in-house technical support. Always have the support team's number handy and be very, very nice to them, because you may have to call on them on several occasions.

Viruses

Bugs are accidental errors, but viruses carry hidden instructions which have been designed deliberately by hackers to sabotage computer systems. They've caused enormous damage, even across continents, because they spread silently and just sit unseen in the computer until they're triggered and set about their specific type of destructive behaviour. That can range from making a simple message appear on your screen, through infecting and corrupting one or more files, to wiping your entire hard disk clean or crippling an entire network.

Viruses get into computers through discs, Internet downloads and email attachments. If you receive an email and you don't recognise the author, don't open any attachments it's carrying. Delete it immediately.

Your computer should be protected by an anti-virus program, which you should update frequently because there are new viruses being created every day. If you think your computer's been attacked, use the anti-virus program to find, then clean or delete any infected files.

Zipped files can't be cleaned, so, if you think a file in a zipped folder is infected, copy all the files on to your hard drive, clean them there and delete the zipped version. Once you've done that, empty your recycle bin because some of the files there may still be infected.

Passwords and security

We've all read of ministerial laptops being stolen or left in taxis and on trains. It happens, so you need to protect your files with care. Computers usually come with ready-made passwords which you can change to suit yourself. But you'll probably end up with many different ones for all the programs and functions you use and groups to which you belong.

When you choose a password, make it easy for you to remember but difficult for others to crack. Make it a combination of alphanumeric and special letters because they're harder to hack into than normal words or numbers. For example, instead of using the word 'idiot', type it as '1d10t'.

Some systems ask you to change your passwords every few months. The easiest way of doing this is to add a number to the front or end of the one you're using.

Don't write your passwords down but make a note which helps you to remember them. If, for example, you're using your mother's birthday, your note could read mumbd, and if it's her birthday written backwards, write mumdb.

brilliant tip

Set passwords for when you first switch on your computer, on confidential documents, and on your screensaver. If in doubt, create a password. And if you ever suspect someone knows one or more of the ones you've set, change them right away.

Organising your work and keeping it safe

If your computer's damaged, it can be mended, and if it's lost or stolen, it can be replaced. But if your work is lost or gets corrupted, it's gone for good. So you must make certain you look after your data. If you don't, weeks or even months of work can vanish in a split second. That's why you must protect your work at all times.

- Set up autosave. For Word files you do this using the Tools menu and choosing 'Options', then 'Save' and ticking the appropriate boxes. Your document will be saved automatically every few minutes.

- Save your work after every paragraph and every time you finish something important.

- Make sure the names you give your files are clear and help you to identify what's in them easily.

- Organise your documents efficiently by creating folders for each type of work you do and saving the appropriate files in each one. In Windows Explorer you can sort files by name, size, type and the date they were last modified.

brilliant tip

Sometimes, you'll work on a document over many days, or even weeks. Other people may be working on it too, so it's important to be sure that, when you open it, you're working on the latest version, with all the updates that have been made to it. To do this, each time you close a document add a number after its name. For example, River project 1.doc, River project 2.doc and so on. If everyone does this, the most up-to-date version will be the one with the highest number.

Storage devices

Hard drives hold vast amounts of information, so, if something serious does go wrong or a laptop is lost, all the data vanishes. That's why you must make copies of all your files, so that you can access them on another computer if necessary. Where you copy it to will depend on how much memory you need and how easy you want it to be to retrieve it, but there are three main storage options:

● the computer's hard drive, which it where it goes when you save it normally;

● an office network (if your company has one), where you can set up a personal folder in which you can save all your work;

● some form of external memory, such as an external hard drive, CD-ROM, DVD or flash drive.

The Internet

To get online you need a modem, a browser, such as Internet Explorer, Google Chrome, Mozilla Firefox or Safari, and an account with a service provider.

We all know the power and value of the Internet, whether it comes to searching for information, using emails, or interacting with others in online groups and networks. Be careful, though, to check your company's policy on using it at work, and make sure you never use a work computer to access inappropriate sites.

brilliant tip

If your connection's slow, try logging on when there's less traffic. For example, don't use local sites first thing in the morning or at lunchtime. Remember the time difference when you're visiting foreign sites and, if you're accessing American pages from Europe, do it in the morning when the USA's still sleeping.

The intranet

An intranet is similar to the Internet, but access to it is restricted to the employees of the company that's set it up. It deals only with issues and information specific to the company and its employees. Not all companies have an intranet. If yours does, you may need a password to access it, so get one and find out about it as soon as you can; it's a really useful source of inside information. If you want to log on to it from home, you'll need Internet access, the appropriate office software, and a password to get on to the network.

 **recap**

- Staying safe and healthy at your workstation.
- Tips on using the most common pieces of technological equipment.
- How to deal with such common problems as losing files, computers crashing, bugs and viruses.
- The importance of passwords and backups.
- The value of the Internet and intranets.

CHAPTER 4

Writing in the office

We spoke in Chapter 1 about the importance of first impressions and that applies in areas other than face-to-face contact. For example, everything you write conveys an impression of you, revealing you as articulate, clear-thinking, a good communicator. Or, if you're not careful, the exact opposite. And this doesn't just apply to larger documents such as reports or presentations, but also to everyday correspondence, memos, even emails. If your colleagues have to struggle to understand your messages or wade through paragraphs of waffle and jargon to get to your point, you might not get the sort of response you're hoping for. You don't have to be Shakespeare but you really should make sure you get the basics right. In this chapter we'll offer some tips on how to write well and suggest templates for your letters, emails, faxes and memos.

Write right ...

... is exactly the sort of linguistic flourish you shouldn't use in your written communications (unless your job is that of a copy writer in a PR agency). In business, the aim of writing is clarity, not effect. Most of the time you use correspondence, in whatever form, to convey information; if you do that clearly, quickly and in correct English, it'll save you and the people reading it lots of time and effort.

Take time to think it through

First, think about who's going to be reading it, how much they already know and how much they need to know. Why exactly are you writing to them? Are you telling them something, asking for something, trying to persuade them to do something? If you're giving them information, when do they need it? Is the timing right? Do you need an answer? And, if you do, by when do you need it?

You need to ask yourself all these questions and also think about where you're sending the information and whether it's an internal or external communication because it obviously matters where it could end up and who else might read it.

brilliant tip

As well as getting the substance of your message right, make sure you present it clearly, too. Dense text in long paragraphs is harder to read so, if you've got lots to say, use the first page to summarise your main points, in the form of a covering letter perhaps, and put the detail on a separate page.

The writing

When you're ready to write, don't worry too much about the first draft. Just start somewhere and get the words flowing. You can sort out the style, structure and logic later. Don't just ramble on aimlessly, though; keep it as brief and to the point as possible and jot down the sorts of things you'd say if you were talking with the person face to face.

Start with the most important information and try to keep your ideas in a logical sequence. Include everything they need to know and suggest what the next steps should be – maybe they need to respond in some way, or do something, or perhaps you'll be getting in touch again. Whatever it is, make sure they're aware of it.

Then, once you've covered everything that's necessary, try to take a rest from it. If there's time, set it aside, do something else and come back to edit it later. That way you can add things you've missed or maybe spot things which could be said differently.

The editing

Make sure the editing is a separate process. Use it to structure your ideas so that they flow logically and aren't weakened or hidden by superfluous material or repetitions. Think about the person you're writing to and choose your tone and style so that they're right for the subject but also natural and appropriate for the relationship between you. Usually that'll mean getting a comfortable balance between professional and conversational. You'll find that using contractions (such as the one which began this sentence – 'you'll') and personal pronouns ('you', 'I', 'we') helps to keep the tone warm, friendly and less formal.

Grammar is important but we often bend the rules in speech. Sometimes, we don't even know we're doing it. Beginning a sentence with 'And' or 'But' is, technically, incorrect but hardly anyone notices or cares about it. On the other hand, grammatically correct constructions such as 'I'd be grateful to know to whom you're sending it' may sound 'posh' and you might decide to use the more informal, but incorrect, 'I'd be grateful to know who you're sending it to'. It's a matter of personal preference but, if in doubt, choose the correct version. And, if you're thinking of using humour, make sure it's appropriate – and funny – although it's usually better not to risk it.

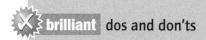 **brilliant** **dos and don'ts**

Do

✔ Avoid writing a series of disconnected sentences, such as 'We need to meet before Thursday. John can't make it on Tuesday. I'll fix the agenda. One of the items will be the new rota. Laura and Simon don't like it'

✔ Link the sentences smoothly to make the text flow so that it's easier to read, as in 'John's not free on Tuesday but we do need to meet before Thursday. I'll organise the agenda and one of the items on it will be the new rota, which I know Laura and Simon don't like

✔ Use plain, everyday language

✔ Avoid clichés

Don't

✘ Be pretentious or try using words simply to impress

✘ Overuse jargon, acronyms or abbreviations

Before you send it off, always re-read it thoroughly. Try to do so from the reader's point of view and, if possible, read it aloud. It's a way of making sure it feels right and it often highlights things such as errors and repetitions which you've missed on the screen or page.

The medium

So far, we've been talking about your style and keeping it friendly but professional, clear and effective. It's also important to choose the right medium to suit your message. Consider things such as:

- How formal should it be?
- Is it confidential?
- How quickly do you need a response?

If it's formal and/or confidential, use letters or memos, not emails or faxes, but if you want a quick reply, emails or faxes are best.

Letters

There are some generally accepted 'rules' concerning how to format letters. Your company will probably have a stand-ard format, so find out what it is and make sure you use it. If it doesn't have one, always use what's called the 'blocked' format; in other words, align everything in the letter with the left margin.

If you open a letter with:

- 'Dear (first name)', end it with 'Kind regards' or 'Best wishes'
- 'Dear (surname)', end it with 'Yours sincerely'
- 'Dear Sir', end it with 'Yours faithfully'.

A letter can, of course, be long or short but, whatever its length, make sure it's well structured. Say why you're writing it right at the start, then add details and facts and, at the end, summarise the situation and outline the next steps.

Remember that this tends to be a more formal medium so choose the tone accordingly. If it's to a friend, you can be more relaxed but use the guidelines on tone and style which we've discussed. By the way, you shouldn't use a postscript (PS) in a business letter. If you need to add something, rewrite it and incorporate the new material.

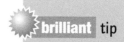 **brilliant** tip

Don't rely on spellcheckers. You may have written 'their' when you meant 'there' or 'they're' and they'll accept each of these without knowing whether they're right for the context. If you do find errors of any sort, don't just correct them; rewrite the whole letter.

Only use company paper when it's company business, never for personal communications. If your letter needs more than one sheet, use plain or continuation paper rather than a letterhead from page 2 onwards. If you're not using company paper, make sure you put your own address above the address of the person you're sending it to.

Even before someone starts reading a letter, the look of it can create a favourable impression. Keep it neat and try to organise your paragraphs so that they're more or less the same size and each one deals with just one specific point. Make sure you've got the details of the person's name, title and address exactly right and check carefully for mistakes in spelling, punctuation and grammar.

It's important to keep a copy of every letter you send.

When you receive a letter, always reply to it within five working days, even if you're just saying you got it and are dealing with it. Make a note of the reference on it and use it in your replies or in other letters on the same subject.

brilliant dos and don'ts

Do

✔ Go for formality rather than informality if you're not sure how to address the person you're writing to

✔ Choose an impersonal opening and complementary close (Dear Sir/Yours faithfully) if it's a 'For the attention of' type of letter

✔ Sign off with your full name, even if you've only used the recipient's first name (Dear Helen, Dear John) at the start

✔ Write your signature by hand and make sure it's legible

Don't

✘ Use Dear Sir/Madam unless there really is no way of finding out the name of the person you're writing to

✘ Use only the first name unless you know the person very well

✘ Abbreviate dates (12 Feb or 12/2/11). Write them out in full (12 February 2011)

Letter template

Pearson Education Ltd
Edinburgh Gate, Harlow, Essex CM20 2JE Tel. +44 (0)1279 623623

Leave 4/5 lines

Our Ref jm/bk
Leave 1 line
Your Ref cf/lb
Leave 1 line
17 June 2011
Leave 1 line
FOR THE ATTENTION OF MR L. BAXTER

Leave 2/3 lines

Yellow Company
3 Lynchfield Road
London E1 5SD

Leave 2/3 lines

Dear Sir,
Leave 1 line
Re. SEPTEMBER MARKETING CAMPAIGN
Leave 1 line
Could you please take a look at the enclosed Media Bookings and Ad Schedule. We need to get them signed off by the end of this week, so if you have any queries please either email me (Jeff.McIntosh@yellow.com) or give me a call (01279 623623). If I have not heard from you by Friday, I will assume that you are satisfied with them.
Leave 1 line
Yours faithfully,

Leave 5/6 lines

Jeff McIntosh

Jeff McIntosh
Account Manager
Leave 2 lines

Encs (1) Media Bookings (2) Ad Schedule
Leave 2 lines

Copy to John Mannings, Fiona Bristow

Faxes

Whenever you send a fax, you should always attach a one-page cover note to it. That'll make sure it gets to the right person and they know who they have to contact and how to contact you if there are any problems. It's not unusual, for example, for one or more pages to go missing or be illegible. So, if there's a company template for cover notes, use it; if not, set up your own. It should include:

- the name of the person it's being sent to;
- your own name and contact details;
- information about what's in the fax;
- and a brief note.

Fax cover note template

Recipient's details	Sender's details
To: Alex Hood	**From: Isobel Wilson**
Company: Yellow Publishers	**Tel: 020 7123 4567**
Fax: 020 7844 8444	**Fax: 020 7234 5678**

Date:	1 July 2011
Subject:	Focus Group findings
Status:	Urgent
Number of pages:	Cover +12

Alex,

Could you please take a look at the findings from the two Focus Groups and let me know what you think before next Wednesday? I'm keen to present the findings to senior management and would appreciate your comments.

If you have any queries regarding them, please don't hesitate to contact me.

Best regards,
Isobel

Emails

There's no doubt that emails have made communications, both business and personal, easier and faster. Equally, they've sometimes led to embarrassing and even catastrophic results, so treat them with respect and be careful. Never send anything that you wouldn't be prepared to say to someone face to face and, if you're not sure about something, don't hit the send button. Once you do, you lose control of the mail and it can go anywhere, including to people you never intended to see it.

brilliant tip

Just because it's 'only' an email, that doesn't mean you can be sloppy about it. Before you send it, check your grammar, spelling and punctuation just as carefully as you do with letters.

Despite the fact that emails seem as informal as texting, you should still think about how you're writing them and what you're saying. Official emails need careful thought; they can be friendly but they must still be professional. And if you're sending social emails, they'll usually be friendly but don't make them rude or inappropriate.

When you've written an email, it may seem easier to send it to a batch of people, but you should be selective and only send it to people who need to see it. List their names alphabetically to avoid offending anyone and, if you're copying it to someone more senior, make sure that's the right thing to do for all concerned.

Receivers divide as follows:

1   To: Everyone who needs to read and do something about the subject.

2   Cc: People who need to read it, but don't need to act on it.

3   Bcc: People you would like to see the mail without the people in 1 knowing they have.

Subject line

The subject line's more important than some may think. The tendency is often to use a general, all-purpose heading such as 'Urgent' or 'Meeting', but your subject line should always give as much information as it can to explain what it's about. It'll help the receiver to focus quickly on it and should also make them want to read it. When you reply, comment on or refer to the message in other communications, always use the same subject line.

Content

Emails are more informal than letters, so you rarely use Mr or Mrs when you address the person in the text. Just write the person's name followed by a comma. When you sign off, use a conversational expression such as 'Regards', 'Best regards' or 'Many thanks'. Most email systems let you list all your contact details in a signature which is automatically added at the end of your message.

brilliant tip

Don't send chainmail or inappropriate attachments to business colleagues. Employers own their email systems and have a legal right to inspect all their employees' email.

Don't clutter emails up. Try to make sure that each one contains just one main message. If you're asking for something or some action, say why and explain the benefits of doing what you ask. Keep it short and don't add unnecessary attachments – the bigger the file, the slower it is to transmit. And if you do attach files, make sure the person you're sending them to has the necessary software and knows how to open them.

Structure

Open by saying what you want the person to do and by when they should do it. If it's someone you don't know, say who you are and how you got their address. Then give them a more detailed explanation, keeping it as brief and clear as you can, and end with a quick summary and an indication of what the next steps should be. It may be that they need to email you back with information or you'll perhaps say you'll call them. Whatever it is, clearly spell out what's needed and by when it has to be done.

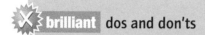 **dos and don'ts**

Do

- ✔ Use both upper and lower case letters; that's much easier to read than all capitals or all lower case
- ✔ Keep it brief, with short paragraphs, and use headings for different themes and bullet points to highlight the main ideas
- ✔ Keep the formatting simple. Not all email packages are compatible, so you may lose things such as indents and italics
- ✔ Keep bullet points consistent by using a dash before each

Don't

- ✘ SHOUT. In other words, don't use upper case letters to emphasise a point
- ✘ Send out spam or any other form of superfluous or junk email
- ✘ Use smileys or their punctuation equivalent
- ✘ Flame, which means sending rude, hostile or insensitive messages. And, if you receive such an email, either ignore it or calm yourself down before replying

Email template

A typical email layout looks like this:

Catherine Jane (+44 207 844 8444)
18/04/2011 16:48 GMT

To: fran.anderson@pearsoned.com
cc: sheila.jones@pearsoned.com
bcc   john.collins@yellow.com

Subject: New Deadline (17 June)

Fran,

I've just had a look at the project schedule and feel that we won't be able to meet the 31 May deadline. A more realistic target would be 17 June. I understand that this may be a problem for you so please feel free to call me to discuss it.

The reasons for the delay are:

1   The delayed response from our supplier (it took three weeks instead of one).
2   The lack of resource at the beginning of the project (we underestimated the resource required but this has now been rectified).

Let me know what you think.
Best regards,

Catherine

Mailbox control

Most of us get lots of emails every day, so it makes sense to have a system for keeping our mailbox organised. To help you do this:

● As soon as you've read an email, answer, delete or file it.
● Don't waste time opening junk mail, just delete it.

- Set up relevant folders for emails but don't just save everything in them. Be ruthless about what you keep.
- If a message you send doesn't need an answer, say so.
- Only check your mail at specific times. Don't be distracted by incoming messages.
- Clear your inbox at the end of each week.

Memos

Memos, often sent as emails, are a very common form of internal communication. They can be formal (typed) or informal (handwritten) depending on what they're about and who's sending them to whom.

First, give the memo a title and note how urgent it is, then open with a short summary of the expected action. If it helps, use paragraph headings and bullet points, and keep it short, preferably on just one page.

Send a copy to:

- people who need to take action
- people who need to be consulted
- people whose seniority makes it courteous or diplomatic to keep them informed.

If there are others who aren't on the main circulation list but who know about it, offer to send them a copy if they want one. You don't need to use any greeting or closure and you only sign it if it's very important.

Memo template

Private and Confidential

Meeting

Due to new expense control procedures, all taxi bookings must be authorised by Richard Carstairs.

Date: 4 April 2011
Author: Alison Burnett
Contact Details: alison.burnett@handbook.com (020 7123 4567)
Circulation: Marketing Department

Using courier services

Documents often have to be sent physically to different places and, if timing is crucial, using the traditional mail service might not be quick enough. That's when couriers are useful since they can bike or fly the papers to their destination in a matter of hours.

If you need to send something by courier:

● Find out if your firm uses a particular courier company.

● If they do, get their telephone number and your company account number.

● If they don't, look up the *Yellow Pages* for a nearby courier service.

● Get a label from a secretary or the stationery cupboard, stick it on the envelope and fill in the name, address and telephone number of the person the parcel's going to.

The courier will want to know:

● your account number (if you have one)

● where the parcel's going, including the postcode

● the name of the person it's going to and his contact number

- when you want it delivered
- where they can pick it up from.

Always address the parcel to a person rather than a department. If you're not sure who the parcel should go to, ring and get the name of someone who could accept it on behalf of the Department to which it's being sent.

 **brilliant** recap

- Preparing to write a letter, fax or email.
- How to structure your message and check that it's correct.
- Writing, then editing it.
- The requirements and techniques of writing using different media.
- Tips and templates for letters, faxes, emails and memos.

CHAPTER 5

Meetings

There's a quotation which goes something like: 'A meeting is a thing that takes minutes and lasts hours' and it's true that they can sometimes feel like that. But meetings of all sorts are a necessary part of the business world. The important thing is that the person who's organising and/or chairing them makes sure they're productive and not just a waste of everybody's time. Chairing, recording and even just attending meetings calls for specific skills; the earlier you learn them, the less frustrating and boring you'll find the whole process. On top of that, it'll demonstrate your own effectiveness and professionalism and help build your reputation. This chapter looks at how to identify and develop the various skills involved.

Making meetings work

A lot of what we'll be saying is basic common sense but there are many things to take into account, from setting up a meeting to contributing to it when you're there. The organiser has to take care of every aspect to make sure everything runs smoothly and no time is wasted waiting for essential people or pieces of equipment. The chair has to keep things moving without short-changing or otherwise offending those attending. The person taking the minutes must represent what happens accurately and concisely. And everyone who's attending can do things which make the process quick and effective.

Organisation

If you're the organiser, make sure you know exactly why the meeting's being called and what you want to come out of it. It may be to solve a problem, make a decision or a simple invitation to others to go away and consider issues in the light of what's been discussed. Whatever it is, keep it clear in your mind. Apart from anything else, it'll help you to decide whom you should invite to attend. You want them to be people who know something about the issue and can contribute usefully to discussions. If you can keep numbers down to around seven, you're more likely to get things done in a reasonable time. Send out the invitations and, a couple of days before the meeting, check to confirm that they've remembered and will be coming.

Agenda

Take care with the agenda. Include all the topics to be discussed and questions that need answering and try to define them quite specifically. It'll help to keep people's minds focused and cut down on waffle. Put the various items in order of priority. Some may only call for a quick decision; others may need extended discussion. Be realistic about how much time to give to each one and build them into an overall time scale. If necessary, arrange for someone to be a timekeeper. It might be worth putting the less contentious items first to make sure they're resolved quickly and leave you more time for topics that need debating.

brilliant tip

Send out the agenda well before the meeting takes place. It'll give people time to think about the things involved and help to make their contributions more focused.

The place

It may be easier for you if you choose to have it in your own office or the one next door, but it should be held where it's convenient for everyone attending. It's not really a good idea to hold important meetings in your own office because there are bound to be interruptions and you'll want people to leave quickly when it's over. So book a room and allow more time than you need in case the meeting goes on longer than planned.

Check the room to make sure that it's big enough and not too hot or too cold. If it's either of these, get on to the service department right away. There should be enough chairs and they should be arranged to suit the sort of meeting you're planning. If you do have to rearrange the furniture for your purposes, make sure that, when the meeting's over, you put everything back where it was before.

Equipment and other necessities

Think about (and find out from those attending) whether you'll need projectors, flip charts, screens, computer links or any other pieces of equipment. Even simple things such as notepaper and pens at each place on the table can make it flow more smoothly. If refreshments are part of the arrangement, order drinks, biscuits, sandwiches or whatever else is appropriate.

If you're expecting outsiders to be there, make sure you give Reception a list of their names at least 24 hours before they're expected. And if you need nametags, ask Reception to prepare them and hand them out as visitors arrive.

brilliant tip

If you want to keep the meeting short, hold it before lunch. If it's going to be a brainstorming session, organise it for early in the morning, when people are (theoretically, at least) at their sharpest.

Roles and responsibilities

Part of good organisation is to make sure everyone understands their role in the meeting. Picking the right people to chair and record proceedings is an obvious starting point, but each individual there also has a role to play.

The chairperson

When you're chairing a meeting, make sure you know exactly what you want to achieve from it. As it develops, keep that in mind and, if discussion is moving into areas less relevant, bring it back to the point.

Before

● Ask people to confirm that they'll be coming so that you can make sure all the important ones will be there. If someone crucial can't make it, try to explain to them how important it is or reschedule it.

Getting started

● Make sure you get things going at the agreed time. Everyone knows when the meeting's supposed to start so don't wait for latecomers. It's their responsibility to be on time.

● Explain how the meeting will be run, appoint someone to take the minutes and explain what the roles of others are.

● If some of those attending don't know one another, make sure you introduce them. Try to make everyone feel at ease from the start. Let them know why they're there, what it's about, how you'll organise it and how long it'll last. Make it clear that you want all discussions and contributions to be free and open, but that you intend to use the time effectively.

Getting everyone involved

● There's often a mix of people who want to monopolise discussions and others who keep quiet. Part of your job is to keep a balance between them. Ask the quieter ones for their opinions and keep the others in check, but stay subtle and polite as you do so.

- Give everyone the chance to say what they think but keep things moving forward.

Keeping control

- As you move through the items on the agenda, set a time for each one and apply it strictly. This will involve you making sure people stick to the point. They may try all sorts of strategies, including flattery and blackmail. They may have thought up their own hidden agendas or organised an alliance with others at the meeting. Watch out for these and, if things start to hot up and people lose their tempers or get on their soapbox, be ready to calm everything down again.

- As you complete the discussion of each item, make a decision about it, even if it's to defer deciding until later. Spell out what needs to be done and who needs to do it and make sure that person knows what's involved and agrees to take responsibility.

Winding up

- When you finish the final item, don't let things just fade away. End on a strong, decisive note. Summarise what's happened and what's been decided and thank everyone for their contributions.

- And finally, make sure everyone gets their copy of the minutes of the meeting within two days.

brilliant tip

In the unlikely event of the chairperson not turning up, always be ready to step in and chair it yourself. Once again, it'll do your reputation no harm.

Taking the minutes

The old joke is 'Never volunteer', but this can be a drawback when it comes to making your way at work. Taking the minutes is a responsible job. It's also good for developing your ability to cut through jargon and waffle to get to the meat of an argument or a point of view. So, always be ready to volunteer to take on that responsibility. And if, as you're doing the job, there's something you're not sure of, don't be afraid to ask for clarification.

● The chairperson will tell you where she wants you to sit or stand. You may be sitting at the table with the others and taking notes or you may need to write things on flip charts. If it's the latter, make your writing easy to read and big enough for everyone to see it.

● It's not always the case but, usually, the person taking the minutes contributes less to discussions. Their job is to note down what the others say as accurately and concisely as possible. Record everything that's said, but focus on key points and words rather than full sentences. If you try to get everything down, you'll never manage it. On the other hand, if someone makes a point in a particular way or with particular emphasis, try to take it down as an actual quote.

● It makes the job easier if you develop your own shorthand. You can, for example, shorten words by leaving out their vowels, or 'shrtn wrds by lvng out thr vwls'. Be careful, though; it doesn't work if the word begins with a vowel, is very short or when the result you get isn't clear.

● It also helps to use numerals for numbers and familiar abbreviations, such as '&' for 'and'. And, just as you do with texting, you can create your own forms for common words, such as 'tt' for 'that', 'th' for 'the', 'r' = 'are', 'v' for 'very'.

 **tip**

When you're taking notes, don't worry about spelling or grammar, just make sure you record what's being said accurately. You can make the necessary corrections when you're writing them up for circulation.

Writing up afterwards

● Find out how the chairperson wants the minutes to be formatted and how much detail he'd like.

● Write them up right after the meeting. If you leave it until later, you may be hazy about some of the things that were said. Use the third person and past tense and keep them as brief as possible, getting everything onto just one page if you can.

● Send them to the chairperson for approval then circulate them.

 **example**

Here's a simple, fairly typical format for the minutes to make the job much easier.

Date & Time:		
Place:		
Purpose:		
Name of Chairperson:		
Present:		
Absentees:		
Minute-taker:		

```
┌─────────────────────────────────────────────────────────┐
│ Agenda:                                                   │
│ 1  First subject discussed (summary) ...                  │
│    Actions agreed by whom, by when ...                    │
│ 2  Second subject discussed (summary) ...                 │
│    Actions agreed by whom, by when ...                    │
│ 3  Third subject discussed (summary) ...                  │
│    Actions agreed by whom, by when ...                    │
│ Any other business:                                       │
├───────────────────────────────────────────────────────────┤
│ Next meeting date and time:                               │
├───────────────────────────────────────────────────────────┤
│ Circulation: Names as above, plus ...                     │
└───────────────────────────────────────────────────────────┘
```

Attending and contributing

Without the extra responsibilities of chairperson or minutes taker, your role is simply to provide useful input. But that word 'simply' is misleading because the way you conduct yourself, before and during the meeting, can contribute significantly to its success.

Before

- There may be some meetings which you must attend and others which you can choose to miss. Your time's valuable so, when you have a choice, find out how useful or relevant a meeting's likely to be before you commit to it. Always contact the chairperson well in advance to confirm whether you'll be there or not.

- Prepare for it by reading the agenda and deciding what you can contribute, what you want to get out of it, and what specific points you'd like to raise or have clarified.

- Be ready for there to be people at the meeting whom you haven't met before. They may want to know your background, so have a quick mental CV ready to answer their questions.

- If the group consists of colleagues who all know one another well, seating arrangements will be informal. If that's not the case, don't sit down until you're asked to do so.

During

- If you want to get noticed, sit where you can make eye contact with any decision makers that are present. On the other hand, if you'd rather not be noticed or think you don't have much to contribute, find a blind spot and sit there. And if you know there's someone there who may have views opposed to your own, sit next to them. It'll make confrontation less likely.

- Stay alert and interested. Have your pen ready to take notes, but don't click it or tap the table with it. And resist the urge to doodle or fidget.

- Treat others with respect and give everyone a chance to have their say, even if you disagree with them. Don't interrupt them or finish a sentence for them.

- Turn off your mobile.

- If you feel nervous, take deep breaths and force yourself to speak slowly. Try to relax, appear confident and contribute to the discussion.

- Remember that all the others are just people like yourself. They won't seem so intimidating or frightening if you imagine them in their pyjamas or doing something very ordinary.

- When you speak, try to share it with the whole group. Resist the temptation to show off by quoting statistics or giving extra information; just keep your points simple, brief and relevant.

- It's OK to question the opinions of others, but don't do that all the time. Leave it to others to point out flaws or inconsistencies. And if the chairperson's weak, help him to keep the discussion on track by giving the occasional summary of what's been discussed so far.

 **tip**

The chairperson may ask for volunteers to deal with some of the issues discussed. It's good to show willing but be careful not to commit yourself to too much.

Business cards

Always carry business cards with you in business situations but don't throw them around like confetti. They're valuable items, not just bits of paper, so be careful where, when, how and to whom you give them. Strange as it may seem, there's a right and a wrong way to hand them out. Remember what we said about first impressions – business cards are part of that process. Make sure yours are clean and flat. Get rid of any dirty, creased or bent ones.

Don't be too eager to hand them out. Follow the chairperson's lead. He'll usually exchange cards either at the start, when you're being introduced, or at the end, when you're discussing the next steps. And when you do hand the card over, make sure the text on it is facing the person you're giving it to so that they can read it.

brilliant dos and don'ts

Do

✔ Make sure the situation's right for you to offer your card before you do so

✔ Offer a card to someone who asks you what you do or wants your contact details for business purposes

✔ Give your card to people you're meeting for the first time

Don't

✘ Hand them out in a social situation unless someone specifically asks for one

✘ Hand over a business card if a personal one would be more appropriate

Buzzwords

The impression created by someone saying, 'Let's keep it in the ball park. If we walk the talk, we'll be ahead of the curve and it'll be a win-win situation' may be striking, but it's unlikely to be one of respect. When they're first coined, buzzwords are useful. They create new meanings and a sort of excitement. But overuse can turn them into boring phrases empty of meaning. They become just noises. Some of them are useful but, when in doubt, stick to plain English.

 **example**

Some of the common ones you'll come across and probably already know are:

- Book time in the diary = Fix an appointment
- Bring up to speed = Brief somebody
- Keep (someone) in the loop = Keep them informed
- Pushing the envelope = Trying something new
- We're all singing from the same hymn sheet = We understand and agree on what needs to be done
- Thinking outside the box = Thinking about things differently
- Let's touch base = Let's get together to discuss something

Business lunches

Business lunches are a strange idea really. They suggest a combination of formality and informality that doesn't always work. On the other hand, they are a way of getting things done outside normal working hours. Whatever your job, you'll probably eat with your boss, one or more colleagues or clients, or representatives of other companies in a formal setting now and then. The context may be different from normal office surroundings but it's still important to think of the various procedures and behaviours involved.

Preparations

Whether you're organising it or simply one of the people taking part, make sure you know what it's for. Are you trying to build a relationship, sell an idea, celebrate a success or thank someone for their support or services? This will help to create the appropriate mood.

That's also true of the restaurant. Choose one you're familiar with, which you know you can trust to provide good service. Tell them it's a business lunch and you'd like a table that's maybe apart from the others where you can talk discreetly about any sensitive commercial issues. Remember that the waiters and *maître d'* can make a big difference to the success of a meal, so treat them well and, if you're the host, make sure they know that. But do it subtly. You want their cooperation.

You'll be eating and discussing business, so make sure you allow enough time to do both without having to cut things short and rush away leaving unfinished business.

General 'rules'

- Don't be late. In fact, try to make sure you're early. While you're waiting, it's OK to read text messages or check your voicemail, but don't make any calls, and don't have anything to eat or drink.
- If you're organising the meal, work out a seating plan before the others arrive. Give the best seats to your guests.
- If you're a guest, wait to be seated.
- When someone new joins the table, stand up.
- However much others drink, be sure to stay well within your own alcohol limit.

Ordering

Don't be hesitant or indecisive. You haven't really come for the food, so make up your mind and order quickly. Avoid potentially messy dishes, such as spaghetti or seafood.

It's probably diplomatic to choose something from the mid-price range. If you're the host, though, let your guests order before you do. As well as being polite, this will let you know how many courses they want so that you can have the same number. You should never let a guest eat a course alone.

The problem of etiquette

Some people don't feel comfortable with the idea of eating and talking business. The importance or otherwise of table etiquette can loom large. In fact, good table manners come down to using common sense and being aware of things that might cause offence to others. For the record, though, and perhaps just to confirm what you already know, we'll go through some of the basic conventions of normal etiquette.

If you're faced with an array of cutlery looking like the layout of a nurse's trolley in an operating theatre, just follow the old advice and start from the outside and work your way in as the various courses are served. If there's more than one glass, the largest one is usually for water.

1 Napkin	6 Dinner Plate	11 Butter Knife
2 Fish Fork	7 Dinner Knife	12 Dessert Spoon & Cake Fork
3 Main Course Fork	8 Fish Knife	13 Water Glass
4 Salad Fork	9 Soup Spoon	14 Red Wine Glass
5 Soup Bowl & Plate	10 Bread & Butter Plate	15 White Wine Glass

Figure 5.1

brilliant dos and don'ts

Do

✔ Turn off your mobile phone. If you're expecting an extremely urgent call during a meal, you can leave it on, but tell your guests you've done so

✔ Keep your napkin on your lap, not on the table, during the meal

✔ Leave it beside your plate when you've finished

✔ Offer wine to your neighbour before pouring it for yourself

Don't

✘ Put things such as purses, keys, papers or mobiles on the table

✘ Touch your nose or hair and don't pick your teeth

✘ Put your elbows on the table while you're eating

✘ Use your own cutlery to serve yourself from dishes

✘ Pile food on your plate

✘ Reach across the table or in front of someone

✘ Overfill wine glasses – two thirds of a glass is plenty

Eating

Different people have different attitudes to the eating habits of others. It is, though, an area in which you can create a bad impression which could affect people's opinions of you. So:

● Try to eat at the same pace as others so that you don't finish before them or have them waiting for you to stop.

● Don't cram your mouth full of food.

● Chew quietly with your mouth closed.

● Don't talk while you have food in your mouth.

What if ...

... you don't like the food? Resist the temptation to complain.

... you have something in your mouth which you can't swallow? Put it in your napkin or leave it on your plate. But do it discreetly.

... you spill something? Don't make a fuss about it. Accidents happen. If it's spilled on to someone else, offer to pay for the dry-cleaning bill. Whatever you do, don't start trying to wipe it off them.

... something falls on the ground? Just leave it there.

... you burp or food falls out of your mouth? Again, don't turn it into a big deal; excuse yourself quietly.

The business element

A lot of the early part of the meal – arrivals, introductions and so on – will be informal and switching to business mode can be tricky. There aren't really any rules but, if you're the host, you can bring up business at any time. On the other hand, if you're a guest, wait for your host to take the lead.

Try not to make the switch to business mark a change in mood. Keep the whole meal as relaxed as possible. It's not an interview. If one person's doing most of the talking, pace your eating so that he's not left with a plateful of food to finish while yours is empty.

It's OK to take notes, but not during the meal. Wait until the coffee's served before you produce your notepad. And be polite to the people who are serving you. If you ignore a waiter while you finish talking to someone, it'll be noticed.

The bill

Arguing over who's going to pay may be fun when you're with friends and it's a purely social event, but it has no place in a business context. Usually, it's the host who pays. If that's you, check the bill quickly and discreetly and leave an appropriate tip. In the UK that's around 12.5 per cent but in the USA it's nearer 20 per cent.

 **brilliant** recap

- Tips for organising, chairing, taking minutes and attending meetings.
- Anticipating and overcoming potential problems.
- Choosing a restaurant for a business lunch.
- Reminders of the etiquette and conventions of business lunches.

PART 2

Business skills

CHAPTER 6

Problems

I f you're faced with a problem, it helps to have knowledge and experience in whatever area it is, but there's more to it than that. In fact, it's possible that these two qualities might sometimes get in the way. When you're dealing with familiar things, you often make assumptions about how to tackle them, because you've done it, or something like it, before. If you look at the problem without such assumptions, though, you might see it in a different way and come up with a solution that's quicker and easier. You bring to it an openness that takes a wider view. Imagination and creativity can be as important as information and experience; where familiarity sees an obstacle, fresh thinking might see an opportunity. In this chapter, we'll suggest a systematic approach to problems which will help you to see things differently and use imagination as well as knowledge to find solutions.

A step-by-step approach

Problems are obstacles to progress and, when we meet one, everything stalls; it begins to eat up our energy, strain our resources, and generally frustrate us. But before we let it start doing that, we should ask two simple questions:

- Is it really a problem? This may sound strange but sometimes problems are only apparent not real. And yet we don't step back and make sure it really is something that needs fixing. No, we waste time trying to fix it.

- If it really is a problem, are you the person who should be trying to solve it? Do you have the necessary expertise or the time to deal with it? Maybe things would get done more quickly if you got a second opinion.

Get a clear idea of what's wrong

If you decide there is a problem and that you should deal with it, don't just blunder into it, take a systematic approach. Write down a description of the problem, using the familiar questions who, why, what, where, when and how, to define more clearly every aspect of it. As you discuss or think about it, you may need to adapt your description, but getting a clear, comprehensive picture of it is a big step towards seeing how it can be resolved.

Show the description to someone else who knows about the problem or is affected by it to make sure you've understood it properly and see whether they have anything to add. Don't start looking for what's caused it – just get what's wrong clear in your mind.

brilliant tip

It's OK to follow your gut reaction about what just 'feels right', but don't rush in and make rash decisions based on emotional reactions or personal prejudice.

List and test possible solutions

You're now in a position to start coming up with possible solutions, but don't just fix on one; think of as many as you can and make sure they're all specific and realistic. Get other people involved; ask what they think. A brainstorming session, which we'll describe later in the chapter, is a great way to get lots of ideas flowing in a short space of time.

Once you've got your list, look at each proposal on it from different points of view and note all its positive and negative aspects. Then get rid of any that are unrealistic or have too many negative aspects, and highlight ones that look promising. Once again, it may help to get input from other people who know about the issues involved. Show them the list of possibles and ask which they'd choose. But don't start finding reasons to put off making your final choice. It's right to examine it all thoroughly, but there comes a point when deliberation becomes procrastination, so decide on the best option and, once you've done that, set the others aside and move on.

 questions

These questions will help you to test the options you've listed and reach your final decision.

Q If I choose this option, what's likely to happen?

Q What would be the worst outcome? And the best?

Q How would it affect other people and how would they react to it?

Q Is this a long-term solution or just a quick fix?

Q Can I realistically hope that this option will work, given the time, resources and costs involved?

Turn the thinking into action

So far, our approach has been theoretical, all based on thinking, discussing, testing ideas. But we need to make sure what we've come up with can and will happen. This means checking that any resources necessary to make it work are in place. If they aren't, you need to rethink it. You should also let anyone else who'll be affected by your choice know what you plan and make sure they'll support you. Be prepared to explain why you think your solution will work; people who believe in what they're doing tend to try harder to make things succeed.

brilliant tip

KISS is a nice acronym for a not so nice instruction – Keep It Simple Stupid. It's good advice, though. Keep your solution as simple as possible; the more complicated it is, the harder it is to explain and the easier it is to get wrong.

Make a plan of what needs to be done, who has to do it, and how much time they have to do it. Discuss the plan with them and make sure they understand what's needed and agree with you. Think of a way of measuring how things are going; set mini-deadlines and important milestones so that you can check progress on a regular basis. If things aren't going according to schedule, be ready to make changes. Think about what could go wrong and have a Plan B, just in case.

And if it's not all working out as you hoped, don't just keep shifting the deadline; try to understand why. As well as helping you to solve this particular problem, it's information and experience you'll be able to call upon the next time you're in a similar situation.

When a problem lands on your desk

There may be times when your boss or a senior colleague asks you to deal with a problem which has cropped up for them. If that happens, the first thing to do is make absolutely certain that you understand everything about it. If it's not clear, or your role isn't obvious, say so. Ask questions and make sure you get relevant answers. You may be tempted to accept explanations that aren't clear in order not to give the impression that you're dim, but this could rebound on you. It's easier to start solving a problem if you understand it fully at the start, and it wouldn't look good if, after you'd pretended you did understand, you had to go back to the boss and ask him to explain it all again.

First moves

You'll want to give it your full attention, so find a quiet corner or an empty office and cut yourself off from the usual interruptions. As we said earlier, it'll help if you write it all down to begin with. Sometimes it's useful to draw a diagram or picture of the problem. That can help to sort out the various parts of the puzzle and make it easier to grasp. In fact, breaking it into parts is one of the first things you should do. It'll help you to separate them all, put them in order and know where to start. If you just sit there thinking about the whole thing and trying to solve it all in one go, you may find yourself going round in circles, having nothing to offer and end up looking incompetent. The quickest way to get something done is to move quickly through it in small steps rather than try to resolve everything in one huge gesture.

brilliant questions

Once again, ask yourself these questions:

Q What do I need to know to solve this problem?

Q Who can I talk to?

Q What other resources are available to me?

Q When does it need to be done?

Q When I've solved it, who needs to be told the answer?

Don't be in a hurry. You may come up with a solution in a few minutes but, then again, you may not. Be patient as you work your way through it and, if you find you're stuck and the ideas aren't coming, take a break, go for a walk, have a cup of coffee. You often find that things are clearer when you set them aside and come back later.

brilliant tip

If you don't think you'll make the deadline, tell your boss well in advance. If you explain what the hold-up is and you're honest about it, he'll adjust his expectations accordingly. If you don't warn him but just fail to deliver, it'll make you look bad.

Learn from others

Not every problem is unique. In fact, the reverse is probably true. The set of circumstances you're puzzling over has probably occurred before, if not to you, then to one or more of your colleagues. Don't reinvent the wheel; it's usually quicker to find an answer that already exists than think up a new one. So, be ready to ask for other people's opinions. Apart from anything else, you may be unaware that your own thinking is biased or blinkered in some way and they won't have the same take on things. The more options you have, the more likely you are to find one that fits. Wander around, chat with people. You'll find that random encounters – in corridors, at lunch or around the famous water cooler – sometimes produce very valuable insights and bits of information.

And even if you're not looking for more options, it helps to bounce your own ideas off other people. You may think you have the solution you're looking for, but it won't hurt to check how good it is by asking someone else what they think of it.

Use every resource available, including people, and stay flexible. You may spend a lot of time working on a problem and then realise that there's something more important under its surface that needs to be sorted out. Don't be put off by that; it's progress, you're understanding it all better, so just accept the new problem and start again.

Problem-solving techniques

The approaches we've been describing so far are all-purpose, general ways to break down the processes involved in solving problems. There are, however, some specific techniques which help to make us more creative and imaginative in our thinking and perhaps lead us into areas that we might not have explored otherwise. We'll look at just two here.

Brainstorming

Brainstorming is a great way to generate ideas in a short period of time. The principle is that a group of people sit around and contribute ideas, provoking reactions from one another which may add to what's just been said, go off at a tangent, offer alternatives, contrasts, opposition and generally develop a whole set of responses to the subject under discussion.

So, first, you need to decide what you want to achieve and get the group, maybe 5–10 people, together in a room and ask one of them to volunteer to make notes on a flip chart. Tell them what you want to discuss, give them whatever background you think they need, then invite them to offer ideas. There should be no particular order of speakers; everyone can contribute whenever or whatever they like. You can contribute yourself but you must try to make sure everyone joins in and that each point that's made is understood by all.

As the discussion develops, the points that arise are written on the flip chart. When the ideas start drying up, hang the different sheets up on the walls for everyone to see and work through them, combining and refining those which are on the same theme and discarding any that aren't relevant.

 **tip**

People are more prepared to contribute if they know in advance what you'll be discussing. Either contact them yourself to explain it all or, better, create a fact pack and send it to them a couple of days before you meet.

To get the most out of the session:

- Encourage people to be creative and non-judgemental. The idea is to generate ideas, not criticise others.
- Don't start with any preconceptions. Anything goes.
- Invite lots of suggestions and get everyone involved.
- When ideas are discarded at the end, it's not personal, so don't be surprised if some of yours are lost.
- Give yourself enough time but set a time limit of 1–2 hours. If discussion reaches a natural end before time runs out, that's fine. Otherwise, warn people when there's only 5 or 10 minutes left, then stop on time.

The success of a brainstorming session is in the hands of the group. If everyone gives free rein to their imagination without any inhibitions, you'll be surprised at some of the directions the discussion may take. Every statement, every idea is valid. It's only at the end that you start looking at what's been said more critically in order to get rid of the weaker ones.

De Bono's Six Thinking Hats

Among other things, Edward de Bono is a teacher of and writer about thinking. He coined the term 'lateral thinking' and he also created what he called The Six Thinking Hats method.

It's now used very widely to help groups of people to discuss and develop ideas together. It's a powerful method and proper training is needed if you want to make full use of it.

The method provides an excellent means of getting people to think in different ways about the same issue. As we'll see, each hat represents a different approach to the subject. The order in which the hats are 'worn' or used is entirely up to the people involved. We think the sequence we use here suits our purposes particularly well. It's a great way of deciding things for and against the options we're looking at.

brilliant tip

Most people have a natural tendency to prefer wearing one of the hats rather than the others. That defeats the object, so try to encourage everyone to wear all six hats for each item discussed.

The hats are white, red, green, blue, black and yellow, and each requires you to think in a different way.

- When you're wearing the White Hat, you should look only at facts and figures. Think about the information you have and the information you need to make a sound decision.

- When wearing the Red Hat, don't worry about the facts; think instead about how you feel. What's your gut reaction to each of the options?

- The Green Hat requires you to be creative in your thinking. Think laterally and creatively about each option. Don't just stick with what's out there already; open up to new ideas.

- When wearing the Blue Hat, look at the big picture. Take a step back and think about each option in the light of the overall situation. What else does each one need in the way of work and thinking?

● Naturally enough, the Black Hat invites you to focus on negatives. Think about the downsides of each option. What won't work? Be careful, though, not to let this dominate too much.

● And finally, when wearing the Yellow Hat, focus on the positive. Look for the benefits of each option.

 **brilliant** recap

● How to work through a problem step by step.

● Dealing with problems on behalf of others.

● Two special problem-solving techniques – brainstorming and De Bono's Six Thinking Hats method.

CHAPTER 7

Research

Successful businesses depend on knowing all about what their customers and the markets want. The way they get this knowledge is through careful research and you'll no doubt be asked, at some point, to find, organise and present information on a subject which may or may not be in an area in which you specialise. So you need to understand the basics of the research process, such as where to look for data.

The process

Having to collect, edit, structure and communicate information on a specific topic by a set date may seem like a big, complex task, but you can make it easier for yourself by using a systematic approach. Like all major tasks, it's best to break it down into its component parts and deal with them bit by bit. Before starting, be sure of exactly what you're being asked to do, the specific subject of the research and who it's for. That means knowing the audience you're aiming at, the format you'll be expected to use when you present it, the resources you'll have and the time available before your deadline.

The objective

Before you do anything else, make sure you know where you're going. Is there something you have to prove? What is your actual objective? Don't just sit thinking about it; write it down.

Jot down anything relevant to it; break it into separate topics, make a note of all the main underlying ideas. The more you do this, the easier it'll be to start grouping them under sub-headings and get a picture of the overall structure with its component parts.

Once you've done that, you can start listing the sorts of materials you'll need to support particular points, such as databases, press releases, technical data, academic articles. Give yourself a time limit to find each of these things but keep the main objective in mind. If you think you remember reading a great article somewhere which would add to your argument but you aren't sure where it was, don't waste time hunting for it. If it doesn't turn up in the time you've given for it, move on. You'll find other ways of making your point.

Planning and delegating

Next, organise your list of topics with the information you need for each of them into groups according to the sorts of data sources they'll need. If you're working with a team, delegate the various tasks and tell the person responsible for each what you want and how long they have to provide it. Keep an overview of it all by creating a timetable with important milestones and due dates for each piece of work.

brilliant tip

You may know someone who has expertise in a particular area. If you decide to ask them for help, remember that very few of us can be completely objective when it comes to subjects about which we're confident. By all means consult them, but make sure you double-check important facts yourself.

Choosing sources

You want to choose data that's accurate and relevant. We'll look more specifically at some possible sources later but, in broad terms, your choices might be between academic literature and the popular press, perceptions of the present situation and retrospective surveys, all of which might be available in a variety of media, from print to sound recordings and videos. Be ready to consult sources with which you may not be familiar; you should be guided by the nature of the material you're looking for.

Even if you're not sure you'll be using all the various bits of information, keep a log of where you got them. If you don't, and you then decide to use something after all, it may be difficult to find and you'll waste valuable time looking for it. And, speaking of time, check how much time and money you'll need for each source.

The quality of your sources will determine how convincing your arguments are. Something that's backed up by an authoritative voice or by verifiable statistics will be far more persuasive than an unsupported claim or one relying on anonymous sources.

brilliant questions

Q Is the author a recognised authority on the subject?

Q How objective is she? Does she seem biased? Does she have pet theories which she repeats?

Q How accurate is the information? Does it appear to be well researched? Can you confirm its reliability?

Q How relevant is it? Is it up to date?

The breadth and depth of information

When you've collected all your information, you should check that it covers everything you need and answers all your questions. Give breadth to your argument by using sources which express different points of view. Ask yourself whether you have enough material or whether getting some more would make a big difference to your work. If you think another article, chart or quote would give your presentation extra punch, find and use it. And if some aspects of your findings have to rely on you making an assumption or giving an estimate about something, make sure it's clear that that's what it is. Don't imply that you know more and never treat it as if it's a fact.

 tip

However useful a piece of information appears, if you can't defend it or provide a source for it, don't use it.

The final structure

When you're satisfied that you have everything you need and that you can support all your arguments, it's time to organise it into a structure that presents it in the most persuasive way. You've grouped the information under separate headings, so it should be easier to organise these headings into a logical sequence, building up to each important issue, proposing arguments for and against, stating clear conclusions for each phase.

The format – proposal, report, email, presentation or other – may have been imposed on you. If so, structure your message and material to fit it and make the best use of its features. If not, choose one which will let you stress things in a way that suits you and underlines the points you want to make.

Readers or listeners should be able to check your sources for accuracy, so include references saying who wrote them, where you found them, and any other relevant details.

 **definition**

Primary source

A database or an article, other document or programme in which an idea or topic first appears.

Secondary source

Any material based on, developing, amending or otherwise relating to information found in one or more primary sources.

Finding data

The wider the range of your sources (within reason), the more variety you'll be able to introduce into your research. If possible, use both primary and secondary sources. And, by sources, we don't just mean books and other media; we also mean people. If your company has an in-house research department, use it. There may also be colleagues who've had to do similar projects in the past, or other company contacts who could help speed things up for you. Whoever you consult, though, make sure you know exactly what you want from them before you ask.

Organisations

There are organisations covering just about every topic or area of interest you could think of. The Department for Business, Innovation and Skills might be a useful starting point for many topics connected with commercial topics but it obviously depends on the nature of your search. You'll find vast amounts of material on specific topics in other government departments as well as in institutions such as the World Bank, Embassies and PR agencies.

The print media

Specialist newspapers, such as the *Financial Times* and *The Wall Street Journal,* are obvious and easily accessible sources, as are business magazines, such as the *Harvard Business Review, The Economist* and *Business Week,* which run articles on companies and business trends, and marketing magazines, such as *Marketing* and *Marketing Week,* which focus on successful ad campaigns and website hits. Other publications relate to specific subject areas, for example pharmaceuticals, music, electricity, oil and gas.

Periodicals, yearbooks, directories and books are all familiar research resources and, if you're looking for books and articles on a specific topic, you can look them up in a bibliography.

Reports and surveys

Companies produce annual reports, which you can access by ringing the company concerned and asking them to send you a copy or by downloading it from their website. The large investment banks are the places to go to get copies of brokers' reports and financial research papers and many more are created by the Economist Intelligence Unit (EIU).

The Internet

This has become the starting point for research of all types. You can access information at lightning speed, and there are so many free search services that it needn't cost you anything. You just type in the keyword or topic you're interested in and, almost instantaneously, are offered countless references to it, some relevant, some useless.

Everyone knows about automated search engines, such as Google and Yahoo!, but there are also Internet directories. They're compiled by humans and they're the online equivalent of library catalogues. They don't have the enormous scope of search engines, but the data they offer is usually more focused, and more accurate and dependable.

brilliant dos and don'ts

Do

- ✔ Be accurate with your search terms. Choose words that specifically relate to your topic but are not too broad
- ✔ Use a second term or an additional expression to help narrow the search
- ✔ Put inverted commas around a word sequence if you want only to find things containing that exact expression
- ✔ Check and double-check your spelling
- ✔ Print out the information because it's easier to read on paper than on the screen

Don't

- ✘ Waste time. Be strategic in the way you use the Internet. It works more quickly when there are fewer people online so, for example, European users should use it in the morning when their counterparts in the USA are still asleep
- ✘ Be sidetracked by other pages which look interesting but aren't necessarily relevant to your search. You can bookmark them to read later

Read more quickly

We all know that reading takes time and, when you're looking for specific pieces of data in a pile of documents, articles, company reports, books and other printed materials, a lot of that precious time may be wasted just getting through the text to find what you want. That's why scanning documents is quicker and more effective than reading them. There are various ways of doing it.

- Look at the contents page so that you can go straight to the part that interests you.

- Read the headings of a chapter to get a sense of the argument it contains and how it develops.

- Read paragraphs by focusing on spotting key words and phrases. Flick your eyes down the page, ignoring small words like 'of', 'at' and 'if', and looking only for the relevant words.

- Learn to speed read. Try to keep your eyes on the centre of a page without moving them along the lines. Read words in groups rather than as single entities, and scan the whole sentence in one go.

 **brilliant** recap

- How to find, organise and use sources to support your arguments.
- The various sources of data – print, electronic and others.
- How to speed up your research.

CHAPTER 8

Surveys

When your research involves collecting input from lots of people, you'll need organisational skills and a familiarity with how to run focus groups, create questionnaires and get the most out of interviews. In this chapter we'll suggest ways in which you can make your surveys, whatever form they take, more effective and more efficient at getting the information you need.

Getting data from people

When it comes to research, data is usually classified as either quantitative or qualitative. Quantitative data is information which can be expressed in numbers, such as the number of clients questioned in a survey and the ratios between those who expressed satisfaction, dissatisfaction or ambivalent attitudes to your company's service provision. Qualitative data, on the other hand, is information that can't be expressed in numbers, such as clients' opinions of the quality of service.

Focus groups

One way of collecting qualitative information on a wide variety of topics in a short period of time is to use a focus group. These are made up of a team of up to ten people who meet to discuss various topics, usually with a facilitator to keep things running smoothly. The ideas they generate can't be taken to represent a population and small groups such as these don't produce much that's statistically significant, but they're useful forums for discussing proposals.

The facilitator

● ... must know exactly what he needs to achieve before the session starts.

● ... asks questions and keeps the discussion focused on the topic.

● ... may be someone who's involved in the research or a professional brought in for her expertise in the field, in handling focus groups, or both.

The scribe

● ... records all the ideas generated.

Group members

● ... say what they think of the various issues raised.

● ... should be chosen because of their knowledge of and relevance to the subject of the research.

● ... should sit in a semicircle, all facing the facilitator.

It's better if there's no audience because it can make group members feel self-conscious. If any others are present, however, they should sit in the background, observe the group interaction, listen to what's said but not attempt to contribute to any discussions.

brilliant tip

Focus groups are only as good as the people involved, so make sure everyone understands clearly what's expected of them and what the objectives are.

If you think a focus group might be useful for your research, this check list will help remind you of what's involved.

1 Decide exactly what you're researching, list the relevant topics and note down specific questions.

2 Decide how you're going to choose group members and what you expect of them.

3 Organise a mock focus group with colleagues and use what you learn from that to refine your approach.

4 Make sure the group meets in a comfortable, convenient setting.

5 Appoint a scribe and collect his notes at the end.

6 Analyse and summarise the findings.

Questionnaires

Another inexpensive and effective way of gathering information on specific questions from a lot of people is to circulate a questionnaire. It involves careful planning but, if you put plenty of time in at that early stage, you'll save lots when it comes to analysing results.

The first stage is to decide exactly what you want the questionnaire to achieve and who you should send it to to get the most useful replies. Think carefully about your choices; make sure you target the right people, otherwise the research won't be as thorough as you'd like. The size of your sample will depend on your budget, the time available and how relevant the questionnaire is to people.

 definition

Population and sample are terms whose meanings are different from their 'normal' meanings (particularly in quantitative research).

Population

A defined group of things that might be part of a study: for example, all UK clients; all suppliers who use a specific accounting system.

Sample

A sub-set of individuals within a population: for example, the 12 clients in Birmingham with whom business was conducted exclusively online; the 40 suppliers who have upgraded to version 2.3 of the system.

Designing the questionnaire

We'll talk about the different types of questions you can use later but, right from the start, you need to decide the best format for getting you the type of information you're looking for. The format will also depend on the form you'd like the responses to be in – electronic, written on paper or spoken over the phone. These may depend on the budget you have, the time available but also how sensitive the questions are. Make sure you have a clear idea of all these things before you start.

Think long and hard about your questions and phrase them in such a way that they'll get answers which provide all the information you need. As well as shaping the individual questions, arrange them in the best sequence for your purposes. Remember that open-ended questions are very hard to summarise, so keep them to a minimum. And make sure that you've designed it all in a way that makes it easier for you to collate the information you get.

Answers to closed questions are much easier to summarise than answers to open questions. They provide data which you can interpret numerically, whereas asking for opinions or general attitudes (which is the nature of open questions) can leave you with lots to read and no easy way of stating the consensus or even of knowing whether there is one.

brilliant example

Closed questions are those to which there's a definite answer, such as:

- Gender: M/F?
- Do you agree with the above statement? – Yes / No / Don't know (delete as appropriate).
- What is your age in years?
- What is your age bracket? Under 30 ☐. 30–45 ☐. 46–60 ☐. Over 60 ☐. Tick one box.
- Which of the following resources have you used in the past month? (Tick all that apply.) Hard copy reference books ☐. Electronic encyclopaedia ☐. Technical manuals ☐. E-journals ☐.
- Place the items in the following list in order of preference, writing 1 for your most preferred option, 2 for the next and so on, down to 5 for your least preferred option.
- Which of the following best describes your feelings about the statement 'Flexi time working is more efficient'? (Circle the appropriate number.)

   1   Agree strongly
   2   Agree
   3   Neither agree nor disagree
   4   Disagree
   5   Disagree strongly

Testing and distributing it

Before sending the questionnaire out to your respondents, or phoning them, you can refine it and get rid of any potential problems with it by pre-testing it on some colleagues. Get them to answer the questions and give you feedback. You can then address anything they've picked up and make changes so that your respondents don't have the same difficulties.

When you're satisfied that it's as good as you can make it, send it out or start your phone surveys. Give people plenty of time to answer the questions and, when you've got all the responses, collate the data and analyse it. As you do so, keep in mind why you've decided to conduct the survey, what you want to learn from it, and what you intend to do with the information once you've summarised the results.

The questions

We've already outlined the difference between open and closed questions. It'll make your job easier if you keep open questions to a minimum. If you do need to ask them, make sure you leave enough space (usually 2 or 3 lines) for respondents to write their answers. Start with general questions which put people at their ease and save difficult ones for later (but try to make them all easy to answer). Number each one, keep similar ones together and structure them so that they follow a natural, logical sequence.

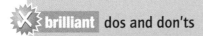 **dos and don'ts**

Do

✔ Make sure you design the questions so that they produce the data you want

✔ Think about how you're going to collate and use the replies

✔ Leave space at the end of the questionnaire for 'Other comments'

✔ Use simple words and avoid acronyms and technical terms. If you must use them, explain them the first time they appear

✔ Remember that the way you ask a question may affect the way people respond to it

Don't

✘ Ask leading questions. 'With which do you agree...?' is better than 'Do you agree with...?'

✘ Ask questions that are open to interpretation. Make it clear what they mean

✘ Combine two questions into one

✘ Use double negatives; they can be confusing

Scales and categories

When you give people choices, do it in a logical way. Put the positives before the negatives (agree/disagree, yes/no, excellent/poor). If you're asking people to put a list of things in order, keep the scale simple. And don't offer them too many options; you want to cover as many choices as you can but, if they've got, say, 15 to choose from, it'll take them ages to read it and may seem altogether too subtle for them. If you're asking them to score a list from 1–5, make sure it's obvious whether 1 or 5 is the higher end of the scale. And use the same scale throughout the questionnaire.

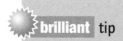 **brilliant** tip

Try not to use odd-numbered scales. They tend to encourage people to choose the middle figure.

Be wary of introducing bias into your questions. Don't call the choices you're offering 'A' and 'B'; use neutral letters such as 'M' and 'N'. And, sometimes, 'non-answers' can be useful. People may genuinely not be sure of what they think of some things, so give them the chance to say 'Don't know', 'Not Applicable', 'Other' or 'None of the above'. This might also make you realise that you haven't worded the question clearly enough, so try to spot it when you pre-test the questions.

Helping people to respond

Since you're designing the questionnaire, it's up to you to make it as easy as possible to fill out. Keep it as short as possible, only ask questions that are really necessary and make sure the instructions about completing it are clear. Respondents should know whether you want them to tick boxes, circle responses, delete things which don't apply or whatever other action is appropriate. Pre-testing on 5–10 people before you send it out will help you to pick up any potential problem areas. A cover memo on one page should anticipate all the who, why, where, when and how questions about the questionnaire and what it's being used for.

If it's mailed to people, include a prepaid, stamped, addressed envelope for them to send it back and, if possible, give them an incentive to do so. This could include some sort of freebie as a reward, the opportunity to win a prize, or even the request that they get it back to you by a specific date. Use the same incentives whatever form it takes.

Make them feel their opinion is valued and reassure them that nothing they say can cause repercussions for them. Thank them for their time and input.

Interviews

Interviewing is a special skill and psychologists have written extensively about the process. If you use it yourself, you should be clear about how to prepare and conduct the interview as well as how to record the information you get.

Preparation

You can interview by phone or face-to-face – which you choose depends on how formal you want it to be and how sensitive your questions are likely to be. It's important to choose a method which makes it as comfortable as possible for the interviewee. Face-to-face interviews may provide more information in that you can be aware of body language as well as what's said. On the other hand, people feel less vulnerable on the phone.

Your choice of interviewee is equally important. Find out as much as you can about them beforehand, what their area of responsibility is, what influence they have, whether they're seen as having a particular bias about certain topics. It helps if you know what's going on in their part of the company and any initiatives they've been involved in. They're more likely to answer your questions if they see that you're well informed.

Be very careful how you word your questions. You want them to provide the information you need to make a decision but, equally, they should seem part of a conversation rather than an inquisition. Try to anticipate any potential problem areas and plan how you'll deal with them if they arise.

Don't jump from topic to topic and back again; group together everything you want to ask about a specific subject, then move smoothly to the next. Start with more familiar, impersonal things and make sure they feel comfortable and open before you progress to more complex and debatable issues.

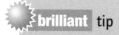 **brilliant** tip

Another consideration when framing your questions is that of time. Be realistic; don't draw up a list which you won't be able to cover in the time available. Make sure the sequence in which you ask things will provide answers on all the important issues before it's too late.

When the person's agreed to be interviewed, send him details of when and where you'll meet, who else (if anyone) will be there, how long you expect it to last, and the topics you hope to cover. About 3 or 4 working days before the set date, send a gentle email reminder of it all.

The interview itself

The interviewee is giving up time for you so make sure you arrive early. Give yourself plenty of time to get there and if, for any reason, you think you'll be delayed, call and say so. But make sure there's a good reason for it. Thank him for coming, introduce yourself and any others who are there, then spend the first few minutes establishing a rapport and making him feel as relaxed as possible.

When you get down to business, tell him what the interview's about, what you hope to achieve with it and how you'll be handling it. It's important, too, that he knows what you'll be doing with any information he gives you. As you ask your questions, keep your language simple, but make sure you don't sound patronising. Listen carefully to his replies; paraphrase them if necessary to make sure you've understood him correctly.

 **brilliant tip**

You'll probably find that time gallops by, so be aware of it, without looking ostentatiously at your watch, and speed things up a little if it looks as if you may overrun. Make sure the most important questions get asked.

When you've finished, tie up any loose ends, go over the main points briefly and say what the next phase of your research will be. Thank him for his time and the information he's given you and ask if he minds you calling him with follow-up questions, if necessary. Exchange contact details and, later that day or on the following day, send him a note or email expressing your appreciation and thanking him for his cooperation.

Documenting the information afterwards

The first note should say when and where the meeting took place and who was there. Thereafter, if you number your questions and use those numbers for note taking, it'll make it easier to understand what you've written. You'll need to write quickly but accurately, so try to develop that specific skill. Keep it as neat and legible as you can and, if you leave something out, try to fill it in when you can. You want to record the points that are made and any special quotations which have particular relevance. Never put your note pad on the desk; keep it in your lap.

Try to develop your questioning techniques.

● To encourage the interviewee to answer, start with broad questions, such as: 'Tell me about … ', 'Describe … ', then move to the Who? What? Where? When? How? forms which will give you more detail. Be careful about asking Why? though, because this can lead to subjective answers which produce opinions rather than information.

- To get him to expand on the information he's giving, put him at ease with gentle, coaxing questions, such as: 'What d'you think about … ?', 'Would you like to say more about … ?', 'Is it possible that … ?' But make sure you don't lead him and put words in his mouth.

- If he begins to wander away from the topic, just ease him gently back to the subject with suggestions such as: 'Can we talk about … ?', 'Would you like to talk about … now?', or 'That point you made earlier, can you expand on it a little?'

brilliant tip

Arrange your schedule so that you have time to write your notes up immediately after the interview, while what's been said is still fresh in your mind.

If you're conducting the interview by phone, introduce yourself, say why you're calling and how long it's likely to take. Make sure it's OK for him to take the call at that time and, if it isn't, offer to call back at a more convenient time. Be friendly and open, speak clearly and distinctly and don't let long silences develop – always give little clues to show that you're listening.

brilliant recap

- The make-up and purpose of focus groups and the responsibilities of those taking part.
- Designing and conducting questionnaires and collating and summarising their results.
- Preparing, conducting and documenting interviews.

CHAPTER 9

Number crunching

Whatever the job you're doing, it's useful – maybe even essential – to know how numbers work and what the various terms associated with them mean. If you're faced with a problem, you need to focus on it, not worry about your ignorance of the figures or amounts before you, so it makes sense to try to improve your numeracy right from the start. And if your reaction to that is, 'I've never been any good at maths', don't worry; we'll look at some of the basics and help you to feel more comfortable with elements such as budgets and spreadsheets.

Numbers

As with almost all topics, it helps to separate out the different aspects of numbers rather than try to cope with all their complexities at the same time. Here, we won't be trying to create a comprehensive guide to all things mathematical, but we will look at some of the areas which frequently seem difficult or confusing, and suggest ways of handling them quickly and with confidence.

Start with the basics

You should try to get comfortable with the figures you work with and have a general idea of what they're for and how to use them. For example, if you need to do calculations in your head, make it easier for yourself by rounding the numbers off. You'd need a special talent to multiply 7,123,235 by 61 quickly, but change it to 7 million multiplied by 60 and it's much easier. Of course, that gives you an approximate figure rather than the specific one which the original sums would have produced. In other words, there's a margin of error, but as long as you're aware of that fact, it gives you a ball park figure to work on.

brilliant tip

Practise doing maths problems like the one above in your head even if you know the results are approximate. It not only helps to keep you sharp; it's also useful for checking on manual errors that sometimes appear on calculators.

Rounding numbers up and down

If a decimal figure ends in a 4 or less, round it down to the lower number. For example, 2.4 is written as 2.0, not 3.0. If it ends in a 5 or higher, it should be rounded up – 2.5 becomes 3.0, not 2.0. The same rule applies if there are lots of decimal points – just keeping rounding up or down as appropriate. If we start with 1.90735, the sequence works like this 1.90735 = 1.9074 = 1.907 = 1.91 = 1.9 = 2.

Get the signs right

- \> means 'is greater than', as in 6 > 4. The sign narrows down to indicate that the second number is smaller.
- If you turn it round, as in 4 < 6, the sign broadens out to show that, this time, the second number is larger.
- ≤ means 'is less than or equal to'.
- ≠ means 'is not equal to'.
- ≅ means 'is approximately equal to'.

Algebra

Some people seem to think algebra is a sort of abstract, mysterious thing. In fact, it can be a great way to solve complex problems. We're not talking about those blackboard-filling equations that feature on TV documentaries, but basic techniques that reduce problems to very simple, manageable terms in a formula. If you're working out profits, for example, you know that you have to subtract what you spend from what you earn, so Profit = Revenue minus Expenditure, or $P = R - E$. As long as you know two of the variables, you can always find the other by expressing the formula in different ways, such as $R = P + E$, or $E = P + R$.

 **definition**

Constants

Numbers whose values never change, such as the speed of light or *pi* (π).

Variables

Numbers that can take different values. In other words, as their name suggests, they can change.

In the previous example, we took the initial letters of the words but, when you want to share or discuss the formula with others, you should use the familiar conventions.

● Lower-case letters at the beginning of the alphabet – a, b, c – are usually reserved for constants.

● Lower-case letters at the end of the alphabet – x, y, z – are used for variables. If the equation has one or two unknowns, they're usually represented by x and y.

- Certain letters are reserved for specific things.
  - **n** expresses the **number** of observations
  - **t** is used for **time**
  - **r** is usually an interest **rate**

Fractions, decimals, percentages and ratios

Fractions, decimals and percentages are all different ways of saying the same thing and sometimes it's easier to make calculations if you switch between the different forms, like this:

- To change a fraction to a decimal, divide the numerator (which is the number above the line) by the denominator (the one under the line), so $7/8 = 0.875$.
- To convert a decimal number to a percentage, multiply it by 100, so $0.875 \times 100 = 87.5\%$.
- To multiply a decimal by 100, just move the decimal point two places to the right – one place for each 0, so $2.367 \times 100 = 236.7$

Multiplying and dividing decimals

This sometimes causes more problems than it should. When multiplying, there's an easy way to check that you've done it right – just add the number of places to the right of the decimals in the numbers being multiplied and make sure you have the same number of decimal places in your answer. In 1.3×1.7 there are 2 numbers to the right of the decimal points, just as there are in the answer 2.21.

When you want to divide, first get rid of the decimal point by multiplying the number you're dividing by by a multiple of 10. That means 0.85 would be multiplied by 100 to become 85 and 0.065 would be multiplied by 1,000 to become 65. Now multiply the number you're dividing into by the same multiple of 10. You then just divide in the normal way, so 1.6 divided by 0.8 is $1.6/0.8 = 16/8 = 2$.

Using ratios

Another way of working out how to divide a total amount into different shares is by using ratios. Let's take a simple example in which you need to divide £100 into 3 parts in the ratio 1:2:2. You just add the ratios together and divide your answer into the total amount. So 1 + 2 + 2 = 5 and 100/5 = 20. You then work out the shares by multiplication – 1 share is 20 and two are 40, so the 1:2:2 ratio produces shares of £20, £40 and £40.

Increasing and decreasing percentages

OK, here's a problem for you: increase 10 by 8%. If your reaction is just 'I've no idea' or 'Well, I can do it but it'll take some working out', try this: multiply the number by 1 plus the percentage. So, $10 \times (1+0.08) = 10 \times (1.08) = 10.8$. To decrease it by the same percentage, multiply it by 1 minus the percentage, which gives you $10 \times (1 - 0.08) = 10 \times (0.92) = 9.2$.

Be careful, though. If you increase something by a given percentage, then decrease the result of that by the same percentage, it doesn't bring you back to where you started because you're decreasing a higher number than the one you increased. To make that clearer, here's a simple example: 10 increased by 50% gives you 15 but then 15 reduced by 50% produces 7.5.

brilliant tip

Don't mix up percentage point moves and percentage changes. If a percentage increases from 20 to 25, it's gone up 5 percentage points but the actual percentage increase is 25% because 5 is a quarter, i.e. 25%, of 20.

Interpreting percentages

Percentages aren't always as straightforward as they seem. You need to be certain about what a figure represents. In Figure 9.1, for example, the profit growth rate on the chart on the left suggests that Japanese operations are doing very well. But the actual profit figures in the right-hand chart tell a different story. Profit may have grown a lot between 2009 and 2010, but it's still much lower than in the US and Europe.

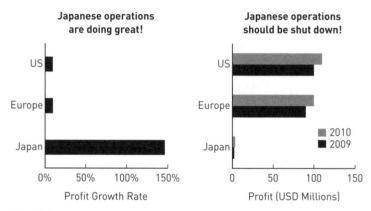

Figure 9.1

Averages

If you have a mass of numerical data, it often helps to be able to average out the figures to give you a workable one to use for rough calculations. Basically, what averages do is summarise data by identifying a value approximately in the middle of a related set of numbers. There are several ways of calculating them.

● **The mean**

This is probably the most reliable and appropriate average. You get it by adding together all the numbers in a dataset and dividing by the number of observations, so, if you have a sequence of 1, 2, 2, 2, 3, 3, 4, 5, 6, 6, there are 10 observations totalling 34. 34/10 = 3.4, and the mean average is 3.4.

● **The median**

This can be useful because it's not affected as much by extreme values. If the series consists of an odd number of observations, you take the middle one in the sequence. If there's an even number of observations, add the two middle ones together and divide by 2. So, for the sequence 1, 2, 2, 2, 3, 3, 4, 5, 6, 6, the median is 3.

Standard deviation

An average is more useful if you know how widely the various values are dispersed. Two different data series could have the same mean but very different dispersions. In one, all the numbers in the series could be at or close to the mean. For example, the average salary in a company could be £15,000 with a dispersion of £12,000–£18,000. In another, there might be the same average salary of £15,000, but with a dispersion of £5,000–£150,000. The mean is at £15,000 because there are lots of salaries below it but very few above it.

This spread or dispersion of values is measured by standard deviation – a low one means that data are clustered tightly around the mean; a high one means they're more widespread.

Budgets

When we think of budgets, we often see them as things which prevent or restrict us from doing what we want to do, things which take up time and are just invented by accountants. That's obviously false. Budgets help you to keep track of things, to make sure costs and estimates are reasonable and keep a balance between what you spend on different tasks, activities and equipment. Even if your own job doesn't involve them, it's useful to know how they're created because you may well have to draw one up at some point in your career and, anyway, you need to know the thinking behind them.

First things first

When you're creating a budget, find out from your boss how much detail he wants you to provide, then start collecting information. A copy of the previous year's budget, which has been updated with what actually happened, will tell you how, where, when and why money is spent in your department. If you can't get hold of it, get a copy of the accounts.

Start by making a couple of lists. The first should show all of your expenses and sources of revenue. Find out the right people to go to for the information, ask for their help and give them plenty of time to find and give you the relevant material. You're asking them a favour, so be polite. These are the figures on which you'll base your own estimates of what you need, so make them as accurate as possible. The second list should be of any risks or other things which might adversely affect the budget you set; these could be internal, such as circumstances which limit the funds available to you, or external, such as a downturn in the marketplace.

brilliant tip

If your company or department has a standard budget template, use it, even if you have to modify it to make it fit your needs. Don't just copy categories and headings from previous budgets – some of them may be irrelevant, there may have been changes to the ways things are done and you may need to create fresh categories.

Establish the timeframe

Find out how your company or department breaks up the financial calendar. It may be weekly, monthly (either in the form of 12 calendar months or 13 divisions of four-week months), quarterly or biannually (two periods of six months). If there's no set rule, organise your budget into manageable, meaningful periods of time that suit your purposes.

You'll also need to know how your company or department rounds figures. If there's no standard way, it's usual to round pounds to the nearest hundreds; over 50 is rounded up to 100, below 50 is rounded down to the lower hundred. So £66.54 and £123.46 would both become £100. The same goes for thousands where £668.11 and £1,481.42 would both be listed as £1,000.

brilliant dos and don'ts

Do

- ✔ Collect bills, receipts, past performance data and anything that will help to make your estimates more accurate
- ✔ Go through each item on last year's budget to see whether you need to spend more or less this time round
- ✔ Be prepared to make assumptions if you can't get the data you need. Use all the information you've collected, including your list of risks and other factors

Don't

- ✘ Base any of your assumptions on other assumptions; that just increases the risk of their being wrong
- ✘ Be unrealistic in what you ask for – focus on just what you need

Double-check everything

When you think you've finished, go through every item and ask yourself whether you really need the amount you've budgeted for each one. When people write a first draft, they always tend to overestimate what they need. Check that the totals are correct and that you've included details where they're needed.

Show it to your boss and ask him if he sees any areas where it could be trimmed. It shouldn't take him long and he'll usually be willing to do it, especially as he's the one who'll probably have to find the funds for it. Make sure all your figures are as accurate as possible and be ready to explain where you got them, including those you based on assumptions.

brilliant tip

Budgeting for staffing is a particularly tricky area. It costs a lot and it's usually a significant chunk of any budget. Promotions or bonuses can add significantly to its costs, which could create havoc with your plans, so give it lots of careful attention and try to anticipate possible changes.

Presenting it for approval

You've taken lots of trouble over it, so make sure it looks good when you present it for approval. The cover page should have on it your name, your department and the title of the budget, for example 'Marketing Budget 2011'. Next, show the budget itself on a single sheet in landscape format. If necessary, you can add a third page of notes to explain anything that may be unclear.

When it's ready, think about how you're going to convince your boss to give you the amount you want. He'll want to keep expenditure to a minimum and you may need to argue your case. You may also need to negotiate for time and resources as well as money. Keep all the data you collected in easy-to-read notes in case he asks you where you got the figures you're quoting. And if it's not approved, make sure you understand why so that you can make the necessary changes to get it passed next time.

When the budget's become an active document, maintain it regularly. Fill in correct amounts as and when they occur and, if there's a difference between the actual and the estimated budgets, work out why and revise the numbers up or down as necessary. There are almost bound to be differences between the actual figure and the budgeted figure, which are known as variances. Don't worry too much about them; just decide how best to deal with them and still stay on track.

2010 Budget (£'000s)	Jan			Feb			Mar			Apr			May			Jun			Total		
	Est	Act	Var	Est	Act	Var	Est	Act	Var	Est	Act	Var	Est	Act	Var	Est	Act	Var	Est	Act	Var
Revenue																					
Sales of Service A																					
Sales of Service B																					
Sales of Service C																					
Total Rev/Exp																					
Expenses *Fixed Costs*																					
Rent																					
Taxes																					
Other Overheads																					
Variable Costs																					
Staffing																					
Training																					
Entertainment																					
Office Admin																					
Travel																					
Total Expenses																					

Figure 9.2 Sample semi-annual budget

Definitions:

Est = Estimate budget figure

Act = Actual figure

Var = Variance (Estimate minus Actual)

Revenue = Money coming in

Expenses = Money going out

Fixed Costs = Costs that stay the same irrespective of the scale of operations. They'll be set by someone senior in the organisation

Variable Costs = Costs that are directly linked to the scale of operations. You should focus on these because you have some control over them

Check list for creating an effective budget

● Keep it simple. Be ruthless about the number of categories you have, just use the major revenue and expense headings and make sure they follow a logical order.

● Check, double-check and re-check your numbers to make them as accurate as possible. One little mistake could throw everything out.

● If it's a particularly important budget, ask a colleague to look through it, too. It's easy to make a mistake when you're dealing with so many numbers and reading over material with which you've become very familiar.

● Be consistent with numbers. Always use the same number of decimal places. Try to highlight the numbers that are most important.

● Make sure it's complete. Think through everything that people need to know from it and check that you haven't left out anything important.

● Make sure it's compatible with other budgets. Check out the standard budgets your company uses, especially if you have to submit yours to a committee or it has to fit into a departmental budget.

● If there's no company standard, make it look like others by using a similar typeface, page size and layout.

● Make it attractive and easy to read and understand, but don't go overboard with colour or gimmicky typefaces. It's a serious document and should look like one.

brilliant recap

   ● Basic handling of numbers.
   ● Using algebra, fractions, ratios and decimals.
   ● Percentages and averages.
   ● Preparing, creating, checking and getting approval for budgets.

CHAPTER 10

Spreadsheets and annual reports

Whether in electronic or printed form, documents are an essential aspect of business. Apart from promotional literature, brochures, tender documents, contracts and all the others, there are balance sheets, financial statements and the all-important annual reports. Understanding them and being able to contribute to their production or to discussions of what they contain is crucial for anyone seeking to make their way in a company.

The principles of spreadsheets

Spreadsheets make numbers much easier to work with and present them in ways that make problem-solving easier, too. Maybe you haven't yet come across them much and don't think you'll be using them very often, but it's worth spending some time studying the principles of creating and interpreting them – you never know when they might help you to deal with a tricky set of data.

Where to start

The quickest way to learn what they're all about is to find a colleague who's familiar with them and good at creating them and just ask if she'll teach you a few things. It really won't take long to grasp the fundamentals of what they can do. There are also plenty of good books on the market which unravel their mysteries and are aimed at people at all levels, from beginners to experts. And, once you've got even a vague idea of what's involved, you can't beat doing some hands-on work yourself. Look at the different options on offer, try them, see what happens and, if you get stuck, just use the help function. Once you start feeling comfortable with the spreadsheet package you're using, you'll find that you'll soon be more confident about the way the program works.

Financial models

It's not hard to create a model but, if you want it to be really excellent, you'll need to be prepared to take it seriously, give it some time, and practise a lot. It helps if you take a step-by-step approach and give it your full concentration at each phase.

- Start by deciding what you want the model to do for you. That means clearly identifying the problem you're trying to solve and the sorts of decisions that'll be made based on the model's output.

- Sketch it out roughly on paper, trying to cover all the things it may have to do. As you use it, it'll probably change to accommodate new needs but it'll make life a lot easier for you if you try to anticipate at least some of these needs. Building them into the model from the start rather than adding them later will make it more efficient and more effective.

- Start building a structure from the bottom up. Enter the raw data you'll need and, if you don't have it (which is quite likely to be the case at this early stage), give a good estimate of what the figure might be. Make a note of the fact that it's a guess and update it as soon as the information becomes available.

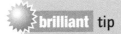 **tip**

Always make back-up copies of your work and get into the habit of saving it regularly, and by that we mean every 10 minutes or so. When you've spent hours, even days, building structures, entering data, compiling the tools you need, you don't want to risk losing it through a careless keystroke or a computer crash.

Be clear and accurate

Building complex models takes lots of time and can sometimes continue long after 'normal' working hours. In such circumstances, it's easy to make simple mistakes that may undermine all the work, so make sure all your figures are accurate and build self-checks into your models to highlight any flaws.

Also, make sure people find your models easy to understand by:

- creating a logical structure for them to follow;
- putting the date and title on every sheet and labelling cells;
- telling them what units you've used – for example, thousands of pounds is written as £'000 and millions as £m;
- explaining all your calculations and assumptions either on a separate page or by writing a comment in the actual cell.

 **definition**

Hard-coded data

Data written directly into a program in such a way that it can't easily be modified.

Derived data

Data which is produced by transforming source data to produce a new result. Unlike hard-coded data, this can be variable.

Effective formatting

Don't underestimate the importance of what the model looks like. It needs to be clean and readable. Try to keep each section of analysis on a single page. By all means choose a style that suits you, but be wary of trying flashy, unconventional formats. The important thing is that people should be able to understand it easily. Use this check list to help you achieve your aim.

- Remove the gridlines and leave the background white.
- Use black font for hard-coded data and blue for derived data.
- Format numbers consistently to one or two decimal places and use commas to indicate thousands, as in 4,300.
- Make columns wide enough for their contents.
- Highlight cells that are of particular interest, such as titles and totals, by changing the colour of the cell, making them bold or italic or giving them a border.
- Either centre text or align it with the numbers.

The Annual Report

There are those, usually people working in areas of finance or accounting, who devour the information and statistics contained in the company's Annual Report. Others, however, may find it less enthralling. But even if you're one of those 'others', it's worth spending time reading it and seeing the overall picture that the figures paint.

What is it?

The idea of it being a picture is a useful one to retain. It's more than a snapshot; it's a complete overview that can help you to understand the company better, see the direction it's taking and how strong it is financially. It's made up of a series of written statements, some of them outlining its vision and strategy, otherwise known as mission statements, others from the Chairman, Chief Executive and Directors, and financial statements covering the balance sheet, cash flow, and income. When you combine them all, you have the story of what happened during the previous year, how well the company performed, and what plans there are for the year to come.

The financial angle

Every commercial business in which the public has an interest must submit financial accounts in order to establish how much tax they have to pay and to provide shareholders, lenders, employees and anyone else with an interest in it with the information they need to determine how well it's being managed. How these accounts are drawn up is governed by both strict legal requirements and informal guidelines agreed by accountants. But different businesses operate in different ways and use different accounting policies, so no two sets of accounts will be the same.

At the same time, the Annual Report is also an advert for the company, showing how strong, positive and ready for the future it is. This means it'll be as selective as possible in the amount of information it reveals; the information will be true but it'll be presented in a way which makes it acceptable and attractive to those who read it. The accounts are produced by the company's directors, who then present them to shareholders at the Annual General Meeting (AGM), and the shareholders appoint auditors to check them. The auditors are independent accountants who make sure that the accounts are a true and fair reflection of the company's performance.

Profit and loss account/income statement

This is a fairly straightforward indication of how the company's been doing over the past year. Basically, it says how much the company has earned, subtracts from that the expenses incurred in creating that revenue, and shows whether the company made a profit or loss for that period. Within that simplicity, however, there's a more detailed structure. Expenses are subtracted in a particular order and, at each stage, they show various levels of profit. Some of the main ones are:

- Gross profit = revenue from sales minus how much the sales cost. This is the figure that management and investors watch very carefully.

- Operating profit = gross profit minus all the expenses supporting the infrastructure and administration of an organisation, such as rent, salaries and energy costs.

- Profit before tax = operating profit minus interest paid out on borrowings for the year plus interest received.

- Profit after tax = profit before tax minus the tax due as a result of trading for the year.

- Retained profit = profit after tax minus any dividends paid to the shareholders. It's this money that's ploughed back into the business.

Cash flow statement

This shows how well the company is managing its use of cash. It's a pretty standard format and divided into blocks of subtotals, each with clear information on the cash movements within various important activities.

- Operating cash flow = operating profit from the profit and loss account which is adjusted for non-cash items, such as depreciation of equipment and assets.

- Cash flow before financing = operating cash flow minus non-trading items, such as interest, dividends, tax and capital expenditure.

- Movement in cash = operating cash flow before financing plus financing such as loans and share capital. This is the cash flow's bottom line and shows the increase or decrease in cash in the period.

 **brilliant** tip

The profit and loss account and the balance sheet are obviously important, but so is the cash flow statement. A company can be profitable but have severe cash flow difficulties and without cash a business can die. Don't confuse profit with cash; cash pays bills, profit doesn't.

Balance sheet

This shows everything that the company owns (its assets) and how much it paid for them (liabilities and equity) on a particular date (usually the end of the reporting period). It's called a balance sheet because the cost of the assets should be the same as the amount paid for them. So the basic equation is: Assets = Liabilities + Equity. The statement's split into sections according to strict accounting rules.

Assets

- Fixed assets are those used by the business for the business, such as equipment and the company's brand name.

- Current assets are short-term assets which, if they're not already in cash form, will be within the next 12 months. They include the stocks held and money which you're owed by debtors and others.

Liabilities

- Long-term liabilities are debts and loans which are due to be repaid beyond the next 12 months.

- Current liabilities are debts and loans due for repayment within the next 12 months.

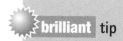 tip

> Another important item on the balance sheet is working capital,
> which is also known as net current assets, in other words current
> assets minus current liabilities. If a company's current liabilities are
> larger than its current assets, it could be on the road to insolvency.

Equity/shareholder funds

- This is a form of long-term finance which consists of the
  amount of investment that shareholders put into a company
  and any retained profit that's ploughed back into the business.

Be careful. The balance sheet isn't a true indication of what a
company's worth. The prices of all the items shown are what
the company paid for them in the past; their current market
value may be very different.

 recap

- How to understand spreadsheets and how to design and present
  your own.
- What the Annual Report indicates and an explanation of its
  various features, especially those relating to finance.

CHAPTER 11

Presentations

Faced with the need to give a presentation, people react in different ways. At one end of the scale, the response may be blind panic, at the other, there's a feeling of excitement at the chance to make a name for yourself. Both are understandable because speaking in public – even if only to a small group of people you know – can be stressful; but it can also give you a chance to show how well you know a subject and how clearly you can analyse it and structure your thoughts to make it easier for your audience to grasp. It's a skill well worth developing and, whichever part of the spectrum you occupy, this chapter aims to help you deal with nervousness, organise, write and deliver a presentation, and handle questions which arise from it.

Good presentations

Identifying the important aspects of a subject, structuring them and supporting your points with evidence, then conveying them clearly gives you the chance to show just how good your communication skills are. It can get you noticed and, in many – maybe even most – companies, it's a fast track to success and promotion, so it's worth spending some time honing your presentational technique.

First, though, let's look at what constitutes a 'good' presentation. In general terms, we can say that it:

- makes its main point right away;
- sticks to the point and isn't too long;
- is well structured, making it easy to understand and follow;
- and, if it's presented orally, sounds good.

brilliant examples

Here are two examples of communication, one good, one bad; which would you rather receive?

- John,

  I have just had a look at the schedule for Project X and there is no way that we are going to meet the deadline. We are already about three weeks behind and, given the way things are and the various objections that have come up, it is unlikely that we will be able to do enough to catch up in time. As you know, Mary, who has been working on the accounts, is due to go on maternity leave next week and her absence will be bound to put a further strain on the workload for all of us. Last week, I remember you saying you felt there was a sort of negative atmosphere and that people were showing the strain. And you're right – team morale is at an all time low, people are stressed out and upset that they have so much to do and so little time to do it in. So, for these and other reasons, I feel that we need to co-opt another person on to the team as soon as possible.
  Mark

- John,

  We need another person on the team because:

  1   We're three weeks behind the deadline for Project X.

  2   Mary starts her maternity leave next week.

  3   We've all got too much work to do and too little time, so team morale is low.

      Mark

It's not rocket science, is it? Mark just needed to ask himself what the main point was, why it was important and what other factors were relevant to it. So, a good presentation needs planning, structuring, writing, editing and, if you're delivering it orally, rehearsing. The points we'll be making will assume it's an oral presentation but most of what we say about structuring and writing will apply equally to written presentations.

Initial planning

Before you dive into the subject and start scribbling your thoughts on it, take a time-out to get everything about it clear in your mind. If you decide what's relevant and reject the rest, it'll make your task easier and save you time as you develop and construct your argument. Think about every aspect of it – the audience, the style they'll respond to, how deeply you need to go into the topic, what you'll say and how you'll say it.

brilliant questions

Q WHO's going to be there? What's the make-up of your audience? How big will it be and what's their relationship with you and with each other? How much do they know about the topic and do you think they'll be open to change or to new ideas?

Q WHY are you giving the presentation? Do you want to argue a point, defend a position, educate, entertain, explain, inspire, motivate, persuade them to do something specific? Or is it a mixture of these?

Q WHAT's your most important message, the one thing you want everyone in the audience to take away from it?

Q WHERE will the presentation take place? Will it be a large or small place? Will the setting be formal or informal?

Q You need to know how much time you have to prepare it, so WHEN will it be given? Knowing the time of day it'll take place may also affect how you deliver it.

(Q) HOW will you present it – orally with slides, in writing as a stand-alone document, or with a combination of the two? It may be an idea to think in terms of both. In other words, write it out as a detailed paper, then simplify it for oral delivery by removing some detail and loosening the style, so you end up with two documents – one of which is the basis for your presentation and the other a paper that you can hand out afterwards.

Structuring

At school and college, you probably learned to structure essays following the sequence: brief introduction, set of arguments, logical conclusion. But the world of business works differently. Most people don't have time to go through all the arguments to find out what they need to know; if they don't get the message in the first few minutes, they might never get it at all.

The Pyramid Principle

Barbara Minto wrote a book about how to structure presentations. It's called *The Pyramid Principle* and it's based on two main underlying ideas: every presentation can and should be reduced to a single main message; and that message should be stated as soon as possible, preferably immediately after a short introduction. If you look at the diagram in Figure 11.1, you'll see how it works.

● When you're thinking about and constructing your presentation, start at the bottom and work your way upwards. In other words, look at all the facts, statistics and other supporting arguments for what you'll be saying. On the basis of these, decide what the central messages are and single out the main one.

● You're now in a position to start communicating, so you reverse the movement – starting at the top with the main message, then looking at the key points which support your choices. Your introduction sets the context for the presentation and states the main message, the main body reinforces it with evidence, and you end with a summary and an outline of what needs to happen next.

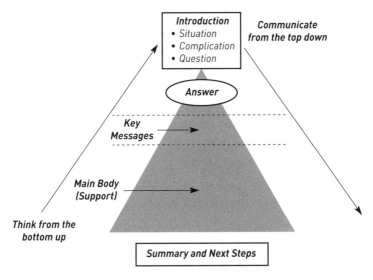

Figure 11.1 A visual representation of Minto's Pyramid concept. Further details are available in Barbara Minto: *The Pyramid Principle*

Writing

When you're confident that you know the broad outlines of what you're going to do, it's time to start writing. At school and college this was a normal, natural thing to do but in offices, especially open plan ones, it's not so easy to settle down and spend time just writing without being interrupted. So, try to find somewhere quiet and set aside a period of time when you can get on with it without others coming and bothering you.

 **brilliant** tip

Don't sit with a blank mind; just start writing whatever comes into your head. It can be stream of consciousness stuff, as long as you keep the ideas and connections flowing. At this stage, don't worry about the flow, the gaps in the argument or your style; keep the main message clear in your mind, imagine you're talking to a colleague about it, and write exactly as you'd speak.

The introduction

As we've already indicated, this is the most important part of the presentation, the part which delivers the main message, so give yourself time to think it through properly.

● You want to make sure you and your audience are on the same wavelength and starting from the same basic position, so state the SITUATION and try to answer (briefly) the who, why, what, where and when type questions. Make the audience feel comfortable by presenting them with facts that are indisputable and acceptable.

● Next, introduce the COMPLICATION that the situation has changed and something has to be done to accommodate that change.

● The QUESTION is: 'what is that something?'

● And the ANSWER to it is the central message that you want to convey. So it's important to get that question right and make sure they understand exactly what you're asking and how you're answering it because the main part of the presentation will put more flesh on your answer. If they don't get the question, the answer and your reasons behind it won't make much (if any) sense to them.

When you give your answer (the central message), make sure it's short, relevant and says what action needs to be taken. Above all, make sure you say it in such a way that they can grasp it quickly.

 **example**

The points we've made about the introduction make it sound like a lengthy process, but this example illustrates them in action.

(*SITUATION*) Beta is one of our leading products. It has won numerous awards and has been the leading product in its category for the past five years.

(*COMPLICATION*) Our main competitor launched Gamma last May and that has put pressure on Beta's market share.

(*QUESTION*) We need to decide what we can do to maintain our number one position in the marketplace.

(*ANSWER/Resolution*) The proposal is that we:

- make Beta more readily available in rural areas;
- launch Zeta, a complementary product to Beta;
- increase brand awareness among the under-25s.

The main body

So, they have the main message, they know what you're aiming at, and you now have to let them know either why what you've said is a legitimate way to proceed or how you're going to set about achieving it. And the best way of doing that is by taking them step by step through a logical argument.

- Try to outline about five reasons (each a key message in its own right) in support of the main message – any less and the argument will seem weaker, any more and you may start clouding the issue with too much information.

- If you're using slides, group all these key messages on to one of them, then write a supporting slide for each. Once again, don't crowd them with too much information. Your job as the presenter is to distil out the essentials for your audience.

brilliant tip

The best presentations last less than 20 minutes. If you allow yourself a minute for each slide, this means your presentation (including the introduction and conclusion) should have a maximum of 20 slides – fewer if possible.

The summary and beyond

No matter how interesting your presentation is or how well you present it, people will probably be glad when it's over. If you've been skilful and clear, you've kept their attention, so make sure you construct a good, strong finish. You should do two things.

- Summarise what you've said by putting the main message and major points on a slide. Don't add any new information at this stage.

- Tell them (and get them involved in) what's going to happen next. Make a slide with a timeline and general outline of what you hope to achieve (with their help) over the coming months. Don't just give them information; tell them how you expect them to use it.

Editing

When you first start thinking about your presentation, you should get a clear schedule for it in your head or, better still, on paper. Allow time for gathering materials, talking to people, thinking about it, writing and editing. And try to build in a gap between the last two. When you've written your first draft, set it aside for as long as possible. That way, when you come back to it, you'll be able to be more critical of it and see more clearly the little finesses you can introduce. The first draft is all about ideas and structure; the final presentation has to be an attractive, readable document. Editing is the way you turn one into the other. Use this check list to help you make your presentation as interesting and persuasive as you'd like it to be.

Introduction
- Is your opening interesting? Does it engage the audience?
- Have you defined clearly what you intend the presentation to achieve?

Main body
- Is the message clear and relevant?
- Is the structure logical?
- Does it flow smoothly between points and when you introduce new elements?
- Is your language appropriate, clear and concise?
- Is your tone right for the particular audience?

Ending
- Is the summary short and complete?
- Are the next steps clearly indicated?

General points

● Is there a good balance between words and pictures?

● Are your font, background, graph type and other presentational elements consistent?

● Have you checked the spelling and grammar? Remember what we said about spellcheckers in Chapter 4 – don't rely on them. Double-check using a dictionary.

 **recap**

● The purposes of presentations and the basic principles for creating good ones.

● A guide to planning, structuring, writing and editing your presentation.

CHAPTER 12

Creating visuals, rehearsing, and beating nerves

n the previous chapter we recommended that you create two versions of your presentation: a stand-alone version to hand out, and the one you use when you're delivering it. The stand-alone should tell the reader everything she needs to know, but your own notes can be a simplified version which you can expand as you go along. The advantage of creating slides is that you have the essential notes you need in full view (of you and the audience) and they make the presentation more effective and the points easier for all to remember. In this chapter, we'll consider how best to create slides and then suggest ways to make your delivery of the material more confident.

Making slides

Slides are great aids for a speaker. As well as keeping him 'on message' and offering a graphic display of his thinking and the progression of his argument, they add visual interest for the audience and a hook on which they can hang their understanding of the points being made. Each slide is like a paragraph in a written document. It should carry one main point and some supporting material to strengthen it. The main point should be made in a tagline or sentence at the top with the supporting statements beneath it.

The basics

Slides can carry words, images, bullet points, graphs – in fact, just about anything that can help visually to communicate an idea. They can also, if badly designed, confuse people or distract attention from what's being said. They need to be created with care and an appreciation of how much an audience can absorb in a short space of time. And remember that each slide is part of the overall presentation, so make sure they're consistent with one another in their layout, colour scheme, and the type, size and colour of your chosen font.

Taglines

Don't think of the tagline as a title for the slide; it carries the main message, so it needs to be a clear, complete, direct sentence which tells the audience exactly what they need to know. Don't try to get more than one idea into it and make sure that idea's relevant to the particular part of your argument that you've reached in your talk. In fact, if you listed all the taglines one under the other, they should give you the shape of your presentation and indicate how the ideas flow and link with one another.

Support

The idea of the supporting statements or material is to prove the point you've made in the tagline. Once again, make them simple and easy to read; don't clutter them up with information or images which may be hard to interpret. You want the audience to understand them at first reading and see immediately how they relate to the tagline.

The support material might take the form of a graph, chart or other image, but the same rules apply – its message should be clear, direct and obvious, without any extraneous or otherwise distracting elements. If the tagline, for example, were: 'This competitor's product is a major threat; since its launch, our market share has dropped from 75% to 50%', your supporting

material might simply be a graph showing the relative performance of the two products over the period indicated.

Make it easy for the audience

If you've collected lots of support material, the temptation is
always to use it. But this can lead to crowded, incomprehen-
sible slides full of stuff which the audience can't possibly take
in without long, careful study. They should be well-focused
snapshots, not essays. Keep them simple; go through your first
draft of each and be ruthless in eliminating repetitions, bits that
obscure rather than reveal, and unnecessary details. People are
there to listen to you, not to read slides so there's no need to
include references to your sources; keep the number of words
to a minimum.

Make sure they're big enough. Each slide should be easy to
read from the back row of the audience. That usually means
a font size of at least 18 points and bold, clear graphics. Don't
confuse people with too many colours – they're useful for sepa-
rating different elements of support material, but use as few as
possible, no more than three or four different ones through the
whole presentation.

brilliant tip

When you're designing your slides, you're using material with which
you're familiar, so it's easy to overlook something or miss out a step
in the argument because it seems too obvious to need stressing.
Check each individual slide to make sure it makes sense. Good
visuals make your job easier, but bad ones can ruin the presentation.
Go for simplicity and clarity every time.

Support materials

Just as a presenter who drones on at the same level all the time will quickly bore his audience, so a presentation relying on the same type of support in each slide can become monotonous. You can keep people interested by varying what they see. Here are some of the most common ingredients with suggestions of how to maximise their impact.

Bullet points

People are surprisingly lax with bullet points. It seems that, just because each is a brief indicator of a particular point, they can just be jotted down without needing to link them or introduce them properly. Look at these two sentences:

- The reasons why profits have fallen are failing to track expenditure efficiently.
- The reasons why profits have fallen are a lack of accountability.

Neither makes sense. They're both grammatically 'correct', and yet it's the way some people write bullet points, as in:

The reasons why profits have fallen are:

- failing to track expenditure efficiently
- a lack of accountability.

Make sure the expression you use to introduce the list fits properly with each of the points below it to form a correct, coherent sentence in every case. Each separate point should communicate a complete thought – don't just rely on catch-all words, such as Plan, Implement, Assess. Restrict each list to a maximum of five points and try not to use too many slides with bullet points. You're there to provide the words yourself.

 **example**

Compare these two versions of a bulleted list to decide which works better and why.

The third quarter's targets have been set to:

- Provide motivational impetus to the efforts of all our export teams across the company.
- Provide proof of the stability of our manufacturing capability.
- Expectations must be realistic in the current marketplace.
- Clients need to be made to feel confident that we can continue to service their needs.

The third quarter's targets have been set to:

- motivate the export teams;
- provide reassurance of the stability of our manufacturing capability;
- bring more realism to expectations in the current marketplace;
- promote confidence in our clients.

Tables

Tables are useful for making comparisons between categories – for example, if you were noting reactions to a new product and breaking them down into those from males, females, different age groups, different geographical areas. The temptation once again is to try to cram lots of information into the tables but they'll work much better if you keep them simple and concise. Limit them to one page and only include essential information. Remember that we read from left to right, so it's easier to read across columns than up and down rows. Put the biggest or the most important column first and order them accordingly across the page.

Pictures

You want them to show exactly what you mean so don't just fall back on clichés or standard clipart images; try to create something original. Be careful to respect the tone of the presentation. If it's serious, for example, don't use cartoons. Be consistent with the style of your visuals and use them as communication devices, not examples of how artistic you can be. It's content that's important, and the form should be designed to convey that.

Videos

Video inserts are great for changing the pace of a presentation, adding texture and variety and making it more interesting. It also helps to keep your audience focused. But, as we all know, technology can be temperamental – well, 'seem' rather than 'be' because it's not the technology's fault. It's up to you to make sure any technology you plan to use is working properly. The more technology you use, the greater the chance of something going wrong – with the result that you'll be embarrassed, seem unprofessional, and all your hard work on preparing the presentation will be wasted.

 tip

A few excellent slides will have far more impact than lots of mediocre ones.

Graphs and charts

One perception is that a graph or chart adds substance to an argument. It shows the statistics, perhaps with dramatic falls or rises, and some people don't then bother to explain what it signifies. So don't use a graph just for the sake of it. Unless it relates specifically to your point and you're using it as an illustration rather than a self-contained argument, it'll add nothing and may even confuse people.

As with everything else in the presentation, when you're creating your graphs, keep them simple. Each one should convey just one message. Make it easy for the audience by giving each a clear, short title; say which units you're using – tens, thousands, millions, pounds, dollars – but don't clutter it up with any unnecessary information or extra notes. And the point of using colours is to add emphasis, not to make them look pretty.

When it comes to choosing which of the many types of chart to use, remember that the important thing is the message you want to get across, not the nature of the data. So, use a pie chart to show the breakdown of a total, a bar chart for comparisons, a paired bar chart for the relationship between two variables and, for something which changes over a period of time, a column or line chart.

Data points

If you're grouping data into separate units, make sure there's no overlap. If your groups, for example, are labelled 1–10 and 10–20, there's confusion about whether 10 should be in the first or second one; the correct divisions would be 1–10 and 11–20. Make all the data points easy to read, list them in increasing or decreasing order and emphasise the most important segment or line. Don't use more than six groups; if you do have more, just take the five most important ones and group the rest together as 'other'.

brilliant tip

Use the strongest colour for the most important data. In pie charts, put it against the 12 o'clock segment and, in bar and line charts, against the baseline.

Preparing to stand and deliver

So you've prepared well, written it, created the slides you need and you're ready to go. Well, not quite. If you're going to deliver it to an audience, you'll need to time it and actually 'perform' the material to make sure you're comfortable with it and that there are no gaps, repetitions or places where your message might be misunderstood. It's a question of making yourself familiar with the material in a spoken rather than a written context. In other words, you need to rehearse.

Rehearsing

Remember, there are three elements involved in any presentation – you, your material, and the audience. Whether your talk is to a small informal gathering or delivered in a 'stricter' environment, you need to be aware of the tone and techniques you adopt and to anticipate how people may respond to your words and images. You can't rehearse an audience but you can make sure you and your material are in the best possible shape.

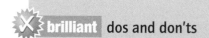 **dos and don'ts**

Do

- ✔ Face your audience and engage with its members directly throughout your talk
- ✔ Vary your language and avoid using the same expressions too frequently

Don't

- ✘ Learn your presentation word for word – it won't sound natural
- ✘ Mumble, talk too fast or say 'er' and 'um' a lot. Noises like that call attention to the fact that you're not actually saying anything and give the impression that you're not in control of your material
- ✘ Wander around or pace up and down
- ✘ Fiddle with your pen or your notes

Make it real

- Sitting at a desk saying the words quietly to yourself is not much use. You need to make your rehearsal as close to the real thing as possible. The ideal would be to rehearse in the place where you'll actually be giving the presentation. If that's not possible, find a similar space and ask a friend or colleague to be your audience and give you honest feedback afterwards. But even if there's no one else there, deliver the material out loud as if there were. Work your way through it using your notes and slides, without skipping anything or stopping to make notes or changes.

- Time it carefully and don't be surprised if it takes longer than you expected. When you know how long it is, trim it to fit the slot available to you. You don't want to gallop through it, so, if you've got, say, a 20-minute slot, make it a 17-minute presentation. It's better to leave an audience wanting more than have them looking at their watches and yawning.

- Don't just assume that everything will go as planned. Think about how you'd adapt if, for example, you had no visuals or were suddenly told that you had less time than you'd originally thought. Be prepared for things to go wrong.

- If possible, record yourself on video or in audio. You'll then be able to look and/or listen afterwards to identity any tics, gestures or verbal mannerisms that may be distracting for an audience.

If someone asks you to listen to his presentation, try to be a sympathetic listener. Constructive criticism is positive so don't say things which may undermine his confidence. If you do spot any problems, don't just highlight them; suggest ways to solve them. Ignore any issues that don't affect the message or the audience and concentrate instead on things that can be improved.

 **brilliant** tip

Even if you're only collaborating on a presentation and not expected to deliver it yourself, always be ready to step in if the intended presenter can't make it for some reason. That happens more often than you might think.

Using notes

Some people are natural speakers (and maybe showmen) and are confident enough in themselves and their material to present it without using notes. If you can do that, fine, but if you're in any doubt at all, make sure you jot down some notes and that they're handy when you start. Using cards rather than unwieldy A4 sheets makes it easier. And it'll be easier still if you restrict each card to a single topic and number them. But don't staple them together; keep them loose. Also, it's important not just to read them to the audience – they're there to jog your memory and keep you on track. So make them ...

- **... short**
  Use bullet points, key words, triggers or cues rather than sentences. This forces you to think about what you're saying and makes it sound more natural and convincing.

- **... easy to follow**
  Use an extra large font size, double spacing and highlight important words.

- **... discreet**
  Big sheets of paper are distracting. It's best if you keep your notes in one hand. Glance at them, then expand on what they say, maintaining eye contact with the audience rather than looking back at the cards.

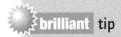 **tip**

If you're stuck for time, just make notes for the opening and closing sections of the presentation. They're the most important times for making an impression and conveying your final message clearly.

Dealing with nerves

Most people feel a bit nervous before giving a presentation and that's not necessarily a bad thing. It gets the adrenaline flowing, keeps you sharp and focused. When you've given several, it becomes easier, but it's still good to feel a little anxiety. The important thing is not to let it undermine the presentation itself.

So, if nerves are really a problem, try using these techniques to control them.

- Use the sort of psychology that golfers and other sportspeople do before they perform – in other words, form a mental image of success. Go to the venue if you can; imagine yourself standing in front of the audience and speaking to them confidently.

- On the day itself, do some exercise well before the event to liven yourself up and get the blood flowing.

- Find somewhere quiet to be on your own to think through the presentation.

- Get there early; make sure you can work the equipment and that you've got everything you'll need.

- Do some deep breathing exercises.

- Chat to the audience before you start to help break down any barriers.

- Don't have any coffee or very cold drinks before you start speaking and remember to go to the toilet before you go on stage.

? brilliant questions and answers

Nerves can be created by self-doubt, but you can overcome this by proper preparation.

Q Will I come across badly?

A Nobody's perfect. We all make mistakes. Just be yourself, don't try to act a part.

Q Will I forget what to say?

A Not if you practise, practise, practise until you know your material inside out. Have confidence in the notes you've prepared.

Q What if they ask questions I can't answer?

A If you don't know the answer, just say so. Tell them you'll find it and get back to them when the presentation's over. Nobody expects you to know everything.

Q What if something crops up which I haven't anticipated?

A Before you start, assume that it will. That way, it won't be a surprise and, when it does, just stay calm and handle it as best you can.

Q What if something goes wrong with the technology?

A Make sure you have contact details for the person who can fix it. If you prepare handouts of the presentation, the show can still go on.

Q What if someone spots a mistake on a slide?

A It happens to all of us. Good preparation will help to avoid it, especially if you get someone else to proofread your presentation well in advance. But if it still happens, don't be embarrassed; just thank them for pointing it out and tell them what it should say.

Performance time

The nerves may kick in a little in the minutes before you have to perform. When the time comes, walk calmly to the stage, organise your notes, look round the audience and smile. Find a friendly face and use that contact to help you settle. Take a deep breath and start talking. Don't rush; try to think of it as a chat you're having with the others there. Stay positive. Don't think of how bad it'll be if you mess up but of how much you'll impress them with your grasp of the material.

A comprehensive check list

- Make sure you've got the latest version of the presentation. As you're preparing the material, give it a version number V1, V2, etc. and remember to put the number on all the slides too – in small font in a corner so that they don't distract the audience.

- Always make back-ups. Save the presentation on the hard drive and a memory stick, and email a copy to yourself. Print it out and photocopy any handouts you need. Don't leave your copying until the last minute – photocopiers frequently get jammed, run out of paper or take ages to warm up.

- If you're having your presentation professionally published, book time with your in-house department or an external publisher well in advance. If you don't, they may not be able to fit it in.

- Book everything you need in the way of overhead projectors, flip charts and marker pens, a screen with connections for your laptop or whatever else you're planning to use.

- Check the room to make sure there are enough chairs and everyone can see the screen. Try reading the slides from the back of the room.

- Make sure the lights are working, the heating's comfortable, and all the technology you need is there and working.

- If there's to be a break for tea or coffee, make sure that's in hand.

- Make a list of what you need to take with you, such as:
  - Your laptop and the relevant connections.

  - All your written and visual materials – slides, acetates, videos, models.

  - Back-up material – flash drive and handouts in case the technology packs up.

  - Details of people you can contact for things such as turning the heating up or down, getting more chairs, sorting out technical difficulties.

brilliant recap

- How to prepare slides and all the other forms of supporting materials.

- Practising and rehearsing to give the presentation with confidence.

- Dealing with nervousness at every stage.

CHAPTER 13

Delivering your presentation

Your own experience of meetings, presentations, lectures and the like should probably confirm that, a lot of the time, the audience is as reluctant to be there as the person who's at the podium. Nevertheless, they're there, they're ready to listen, and they'll be grateful to you if you don't bore them or waste their time. So you should aim to grab their attention, make them interested in what you're saying and say it in a way that's easy for them to absorb and makes them think.

The main elements of presentation

Presentational skills are well worth developing. They can help you raise your profile and demonstrate your capabilities very directly to a number of people. So it's worth looking at the various ways of constructing your presentation and the different forces at work when you're actually up there performing.

Structure

The old cliché is that a good story must have a beginning, a middle and an end. In a way that's not very helpful. If you read the phone book to them, those three elements would be there because you'd start, go on for a bit, then stop. But the three stages are more than chronological issues – they refer to the specific way in which you handle the contents. Make it clear, simple and easy to remember by stating your aims clearly and using repetition to reinforce them.

● For the beginning, tell them what you're going to do.

● For the middle, do it.

● For the end, tell them what you've done.

What we've outlined here is the classic Introduction – Main body – Conclusion framework of most good writing.

brilliant tip

Always start your presentation on time. If key people come in late, summarise very quickly what you've already done, then move on. Don't delay starting while you wait for latecomers.

The beginning

You can't expect your audience to be enthusiastic if you're not. If you start by droning on, mumbling, being apologetic or doing any of the other things that nervousness may cause, you'll turn them off right away and it'll be very difficult to get them back again. So, take some time to create an opening which will have an impact and grab them from the word go. A good way to start is by surprising them with something that's not obviously connected with the subject matter – it could be a quotation, an anecdote, a striking fact or a provocative question.

Once you've stirred their curiosity in this way, say who you are, why you're speaking on this topic and establish your credentials as a credible person who knows what she's talking about. Thank them for coming, let them know what you expect from them in the way of participation, and gradually start getting rid of the natural 'her and us' divide that's built in to any presentation scenario where audience and speaker are geographically and psychologically separate. Make everyone, including yourself, part of a single group. Never turn your back on them and try to avoid using 'I' and 'you'. Use 'we' instead.

Tell them:

- what you're going to talk about and why;
- when you'll take questions;
- whether you'll be supplying handouts;
- how long it's all going to last;
- whether there'll be any breaks.

The middle

You've got their interest and they know the journey on which you're going to take them. What you start to give them now is an argument that builds logically, with its main points clearly stated in the same sequence you used when you outlined them in the introduction. Say what each slide is for, even if that seems self-evident. Never show one without commenting on it in some way. As you move from one point to the next, tell them how they relate to one another and make your links easy to follow.

It's perhaps surprising that even highly intelligent people with reasonable communication skills sometimes fall into the jargon trap or use polysyllabic words to sound impressive. That's not a good idea; in fact, it's counter-productive. Your audience will thank you for keeping your language simple. Use short sentences and avoid idioms, slang or sarcasm, especially if there are non-native speakers in the audience.

brilliant dos and don'ts

Do

✔ Be aware of how the audience is reacting and be ready to adjust your delivery accordingly. If people look bored, ask a question, change your tone or do something to provoke them. If they look confused, make your point again in simpler terms

✔ Give them time to take in the information on each slide before you start speaking about it

✔ Watch the time to make sure you stay within the limits you've set yourself. If you're running out of time, cut out less important things, and if you're ahead of time, don't worry. As long as you've presented your message(s) clearly, finishing early is fine

Don't

✘ Panic if you make a mistake; it happens to all of us. Just correct it and move on

The end

Just as you were careful to link the various points in the main body, make sure the audience knows that you've finished building your argument and you're now preparing to wind up the presentation. Summarise the main points you've made; draw conclusions or make recommendations about what should come next. Make the ending clear, upbeat and positive, thank them for listening and then ask if they have any questions.

Performance skills

By definition, a presentation is a performance. People are there not to read (or hear you read) a set of slides or an article; they expect something extra – the dimension that comes with live, face-to-face communication. You've used your mind to think of and structure the ideas, now use your voice and body language to give them extra force.

Using your voice

● There's a difference between projecting your voice and shouting. Speak loud enough for the people at the back to be able to hear you. Don't keep it at the same level, though, as that could become boring or oppressive; vary your volume to emphasise key points.

● Vary your pitch, too, so that you don't sound monotonous. Don't let it tail off when you're making your points but do use downward inflections. The fashion in normal speech nowadays is to end almost every sentence on an upward inflection, the way we do when we're asking a question. But the effect of that is to give an impression of uncertainty, as if the speaker is seeking approval or reassurance. A strong downward inflection, on the other hand, sounds confident and persuasive.

brilliant tip

The tendency, if you're nervous or think you're boring an audience, is to speed up, gabble the words and generally give the impression that you're anxious to leave. It's much more effective to speak more slowly and clearly than you would in a normal conversation. And don't be afraid to pause; it's a good technique which gives you a chance to stress an important point and the audience time to absorb it.

Using your body

● Some people use gestures more than others. If they're extreme or too repetitive, they become distractions and attention shifts to them rather than staying with your argument. The same applies to fidgeting or playing with a pen. Try to keep your hands loosely by your sides, not behind your back, in your pockets, on your hips or fiddling with your hair. And don't fold your arms – it's considered to be a defensive posture.

- Make eye contact with people, but make sure you're looking at, not through, them. If an audience seems hostile, look for a friendly face among them, but beware of just concentrating on one or two individuals who seem sympathetic; look at several people, giving each a few seconds before you move your eyes to the next. Smile and try to look as if you're enjoying being there, even if you're not.

- Stand up straight and don't shift from foot to foot or pace up and down. Don't let anxieties about how you're moving or standing force you into unnatural poses. Making yourself stand still can look and feel unnatural, so trust yourself and let your personality come through. Be confident and deliberate in your movements.

Dealing with questions

Quite often, when the presenter asks, at the end of his talk, if there are any questions, there's an embarrassing silence. The presenter immediately thinks that everyone's just anxious to get away or they haven't understood what he's been talking about, but there are many reasons why this occurs. One way to fill the gap is to have a 'plant' in the audience whom you've briefed to ask something. Alternatively, you can have a few questions ready yourself. That'll give people a chance to think about things they want to ask.

When the questions do start coming, treat each one equally, whether you think the answer's difficult or obvious. There's no such thing as a stupid question and, if someone asks something, they deserve an answer. So ...

- **Listen ...**

  ... carefully to what's being asked. If it's a long or complicated question, note down points as they arise, and don't start your answer until you're sure the speaker's finished.

- **Be sure you understand ...**

  ... the question before you start to answer it. Thank the questioner for asking it and paraphrase it so that everyone knows the question and you're sure you've understood it properly yourself.

- **Pause ...**

  ... to work out what you're going to reply but make sure the questioner knows you're thinking about how to answer him.

- **Answer ...**

  ... as briefly as you can, using terms your audience will understand easily. Make sure the person who asked it is satisfied with your response and, if it needs a longer, more detailed answer, offer to discuss it with him afterwards.

When you're answering, don't just look at the person who asked the question; include everyone as you did in the presentation itself. Wherever possible, link the question back to your main message to reinforce that.

brilliant tip

When you're getting near the end of your allotted time, tell them there's time for just one more question and, when you've answered it, thank them all for coming.

The hard questions

There are many reasons that people ask questions, and they're not always to do with the presentation. People can be long-winded, rude and aggressive; their questions can be awkward, embarrassing or irrelevant. Whatever is thrown at you, stay calm. If you feel threatened, don't get angry or upset. You may feel like that inside, but suppress it and stay in control. You could ask them to repeat the question or, even better, to expand on it in some way. This'll buy you time and maybe throw the onus back on them.

If you don't know the answer to a question, say you'll find it afterwards and get back to the questioner with it. And, if you do that, make sure you keep your promise.

Sometimes, people ask questions in the course of a presentation before you actually get to the subject they're asking about. If that happens, tell them you'll be dealing with their point later and ask if they'd mind waiting until then. Then, when you do get to the relevant topic, turn to the person who asked about it and give him his answer.

If the question's awkward or irrelevant, stay calm as before and suggest that it would be better to discuss it during the break or afterwards.

The most potentially embarrassing questions are the hostile, aggressive ones. If you get one of those, the most important thing to do is remain calm and polite. Don't give the person the satisfaction of upsetting you. Tell them you understand what they're asking and make it all less personal by looking for common ground between you. Ask them to give an example or repeat their question but without the aggressive edge. Stay calm, objective and in control. Don't raise your voice or get into an argument; just answer as briefly as you can and move on.

 **tip**

Anticipate the sorts of questions you think you'll get. People tend to ask about things relating to their own field of expertise, so think about who'll be there and what departments they're from. That way, you can prepare your answers and even have back-up material to illustrate them if needed.

Team presentations

If you're part of a team, work together to help and support one another. If you're the team leader, make sure everyone knows what they're supposed to do and explain why they're handling the particular part of the presentation you've allocated to them. It should run as smoothly as if it were being given by a single individual, so get one of the team to make sure that all the slides are formatted in the same way. Take as much care with the transition points between speakers as with what each is saying. Each speaker should summarise what they've said, then introduce the speaker and topic of the next section. Avoid clichés such as: 'OK, go for it, John' or 'Over to you, Samantha'.

The argument should be presented in the same, clear, logical way that you'd use for a normal presentation. Repeat the main points and try to arrange it so that team members are all talking about different aspects of the same theme rather than on separate themes. One theme repeated three times will have much more impact than three separate themes.

Be positive about supporting one another by saying things such as: 'Let me add to the point James was making' or 'As Kate said ... '. And, while you're waiting for your turn, or if you've finished speaking, pay attention to others in the team even though you know exactly what they'll be saying. Look at them, not at the audience.

Speaking off-the-cuff

People who are good at speaking impromptu always sound as if they've prepared the material. You can do that yourself if you think about what you'd say before anyone asks your opinion. Don't just say the first thing that comes into your head. Take your time to decide what point you want to make before you start speaking. Silence is less embarrassing than spouting incoherent rubbish or just rambling on. Stick to the point and think of it as a mini-presentation which is structured as well as the full version.

brilliant tip

Jot down examples, anecdotes and quotations in a notebook and learn them. If you can start an impromptu speech with one that's relevant to the subject, your audience will be impressed by your professionalism and ease.

Being in the audience

You'll probably find yourself attending far more presentations than you give at the start of your career. This doesn't mean you're just an anonymous entity; the way you behave can get you noticed – negatively as well as positively.

 **dos and don'ts**

Do

✔ Make sure it's relevant for you to attend

✔ Confirm that you'll be there

✔ Pay attention to what's being said and be able to summarise it all afterwards

✔ Sit near an exit if you have to leave early

Don't

✘ Chat with or mutter comments to the people beside you

✘ Show that you're bored

✘ Ask awkward, irrelevant, aggressive or hostile questions

In the end, if presenters and audience alike treat the presentation process with respect, it can produce some very impressive results, in terms of both the topic it's dealing with and the perceived professionalism of everyone there.

 **recap**

● Structuring an effective presentation to maximise its impact.

● Using your voice and body to make the most of your material.

● Dealing with questions.

● Presenting as part of a team.

PART 3

Other people

CHAPTER 14

Teamwork and team leadership

There aren't many jobs where you work in complete or even relative isolation. If you find it hard to delegate, get frustrated by the fact that committees and consultations slow down the decision-making process, or feel your standards aren't being met by the people you're working with, you'd better get used to the idea that working as part of a team is an essential part of succeeding in nearly all companies and institutions. Your own individual skills may be admired but success will depend on how you interact with colleagues. So it's worth looking at the basics of teamwork and the roles of team members.

The team and you

The basic equation is simple: if you're in a successful team, your own chances of success are greater; if your team underperforms, it'll reflect badly on everyone in it. Rewards such as promotions and bonuses are frequently based on the performance of the team rather than that of the individuals in it. All of this adds up to the importance of being in a good team, understanding what makes it work, and how you can contribute to it.

The main elements of team success

It's relatively easy to identify the main features which bind teams together and make them effective.

- **Shared goals ...**

  ... mean that everyone is working to achieve the same result and there are no personal or hidden agendas.

- **Productivity ...**

  ... is the result of getting the work done, not wasting time, and making sure you meet deadlines.

- **Understanding the different roles ...**

  ... on the part of all team members not only makes their own functions and responsibilities clear but also equips them to work outside their own roles when necessary to get things done.

- **Good communication ...**

  ... makes sure that all ideas are considered and any problems are discussed and resolved. It also means that everyone gets a chance to speak and, when someone speaks, everyone listens.

- **Personal growth and recognition ...**

  ... helps team members to feel valued. In good teams, individuals are praised within the team and publicly for their contributions, and given the chance to develop with the help of a mentor.

- **Team spirit and mutual respect ...**

  ... create a positive atmosphere. When relationships between all members are good, supportive and sympathetic, working together is a pleasure.

- **Staying open to 'outsiders' ...**

  ... ensures that the team doesn't become a clique that refuses input, influence and criticism from others.

Being an effective team player

In fact, the word 'team' is a broad concept. It may refer not only to a formal team, set up to do a specific job, but simply to the fact that you're part of a department or section with other interdependent people, all working towards the same goals. So the skills we're talking about apply in almost all work situations because the workplace is basically a team environment.

Let's start with your personal attitude to work and your colleagues. If you give the impression that you don't care much about outcomes, it'll have a depressive effect for you and others, so be positive and enthusiastic about what your team's doing. If things go wrong, focus on solving problems rather than finding out who's to blame. If others are struggling, help them and, if you yourself make a mistake, admit it. If you start blustering or making excuses, it's a sign of weakness. Just accept the fact that you're not perfect; others will respect you for it.

We've already mentioned the importance of mutual respect. There'll be some team members who are your friends and others you don't know so well, but try to find common ground with all of them; get to understand their strengths and weaknesses and how they like to work. Help them (as they'll help you) by encouraging them and telling them when they've done a good job, but make sure you do it sincerely – if you start getting a reputation for overdoing the praise, no one will believe anything you say.

Keep an open mind to all ideas and viewpoints and make sure you know your own role and responsibilities. If you don't, ask the team leader what's needed and be a real, contributing team member. Don't wait to be told what to do, be ready to take the initiative and suggest improvements in the way things are being done. Let others know they can rely on you to do good work yourself and help them. And if you make a promise, keep it.

brilliant tip

The best team players are aware of the different roles that go to make up their team and are always ready to take on a role which isn't necessarily the one that's most natural to them to make sure the team has the right balance.

Team roles

Teams obviously need members to perform different functions and people naturally tend to choose roles which they think are best suited to their own skills and personality. Dr Meredith Belbin worked out a comprehensive list of roles that is often used in business. Ideally, there'd be someone temperamentally suited to each of the roles but, if most team members have the same type of personality, problems could arise. We'll give some examples of Dr Belbin's roles so that you can judge which one might suit you best.

 **example**

- **Role – The Plant**
  Melissa is creative, imaginative and unorthodox in her approach. She's capable of solving very difficult problems but often tends to ignore things she sees as 'incidentals'. She also shows a certain remoteness from others but is always ready to present them with her ideas.

- **Role – The Resource Investigator**
  Jack is the team's extrovert. His enthusiasm is obvious and he's always exploring new opportunities, developing contacts and communicating readily with everyone. He's the team's networker; if they need something, he'll know where to get it. He can sometimes be over-optimistic and his early enthusiasms can fade quite quickly, but his contacts make him a useful team member.

- **Role – The Coordinator**
  Deborah is a natural leader. She's mature, experienced, confident and makes sure that everyone knows what's required of them. She's fair and treats everyone as equals. Sometimes, her insistence on discussing ideas is frustrating for members who are impatient to make decisions quickly or already convinced their idea is 'right', but consultation usually results in the decisions being more secure. Her tendency to delegate is sometimes interpreted as offloading work she should do herself but it keeps things moving and gets things done.

- **Role – The Shaper**

  Freddie seems to thrive on pressure. He's a dynamic character, loves a challenge, and has the drive and courage to sort out problems and overcome them. His enthusiasm is such that he sometimes hurts people's feelings and he's pretty easy to provoke, but his energy is invaluable to the team.

- **Role – The Monitor-Evaluator**

  Donald is almost the opposite of Freddie. He's always calm, weighs things up carefully and sees the wider picture and its many possibilities. His judgement is sound and his objectivity makes sure that the team doesn't commit to doing something which might prove fruitless. The problem is that he lacks drive and doesn't really inspire the other team members.

- **Role – The Team Worker**

  Isobel is a sort of peacemaker. She's unassuming, always ready to listen and act as a mediator between others. She's a born diplomat and it's thanks to her that the team's interpersonal relationships don't develop into potentially harmful disagreements. She's sensitive to atmospheres and can quickly spot when someone feels hard done by or excluded. It's a skill which sometimes isn't appreciated by those eager to get things moving more quickly and she can seem indecisive but she does help to keep the team together.

- **Role – The Implementer**

  Caroline is practical. She's disciplined, reliable, efficient and can look at a problem and quickly work out how to approach the difficulties. Basically, she turns ideas into practical actions. She's sometimes slow to respond to new possibilities and doesn't seem particularly enthusiastic about others' flashes of inspiration or innovative ideas but she does know how to turn them into realities. She can be inflexible but her practical skills make her an important part of the team organism.

- Role – The Completer-Finisher

  Tom has always been conscientious, careful, maybe even anxious in his approach. He combs through details to eliminate mistakes, fill in the gaps and make sure every base has been covered. He also knows whether the project's on or behind schedule. He's a bit of a worrier, tends not to delegate and his meticulous analysis can be frustrating for others waiting to get on with their part of the operation, but they know that, with him checking things, the job will be done properly and on time.

- Role – The Specialist

  Val brings to the team specific knowledge of a particular area. She's single-minded, dedicated and doesn't need any prompting to get on with her work. Because of her specialisation, she tends to focus on its technicalities and her contributions are restricted to her area of expertise, but the team relies on her specialised knowledge and rare skills to make sure the outcomes are of high quality.

Leading a team

All team players are important but the role of leader obviously calls for specific skills. Some people are happy not to have the responsibility; others jump at the chance. There certainly are natural leaders but there are also plenty of examples of people who may not have seemed so but who have worked to develop their leadership skills. There's no one way of leading – different personalities encourage different techniques, and the members of one team may respond differently from members of another. The more you work in teams, the more aware you'll become of how the leader has to change and adapt.

The leader's responsibilities

- **Understand the job**

  As leader, if you don't understand the job, the chance of your team doing it properly are slim. So make sure you know exactly what needs to be done, plan how you're going to do it and prioritise your various goals. Don't take on, for yourself or any of your team members, an excessive workload. If it means saying no to people in the organisation who are senior to you, don't be afraid to do so. Part of your responsibility is to make sure your team members have a good work/life balance.

● **Delegate**
Discuss what's needed by individual members and the team as a whole, then, in the light of their skills, their workloads and their needs in terms of growth and development, decide who's going to do what. Take the time to explain the whole project as well as their part in it; let them know exactly what you want from each of them and make sure they understand it. Try not to tell them how to do it; give them the scope and freedom to decide that for themselves.

● **Motivate**
Good team spirit is crucial. Encourage people to work for the team, not just for themselves. Get them all involved and agreed on the overall goal, wherever they are in the hierarchy. Find out what motivates them and use that to keep them interested.

● **Help team members to develop**
Give them plenty of feedback on their work, help them to see where they could improve and give them opportunities to show that they can. Always support them, especially when something's gone wrong or the job is proving difficult. Don't jump on their mistakes; show that you understand them, that these things happen and that they can easily be put right. The best policy is not criticism but encouragement.

● **Deal with problems sensitively**
Keep the team happy by sorting out any problems – internal or external – as soon as they arise. Avoid and discourage any sort of confrontation and get everyone to work things out together. When you're commenting on something that's happened, just stick to the facts; don't make judgements. Rather than make statements yourself about the issue, ask

them questions – that way, the problems and potential solutions will come from them and it won't sound as if you're being critical. And, if whatever it is is the result of a mistake by a team member, find a way of dealing with it without making him feel bad or stupid.

- **Meet your deadlines**
  Make sure everyone knows how long they have to finish the job. Sometimes, some team members may have to wait for others to finish their tasks before they can continue with their own. If you create a context in which everyone can be honest and open in their communications, they'll be able to raise issues such as these freely and resolve them more quickly.

- **Monitor quality**
  All the way through the job, keep a check on how it's progressing, making sure that in all its aspects everyone is sticking to the high standards on which you've all agreed.

- **Represent your team**
  As well as letting the team itself know how work is progressing, perhaps in weekly status meetings, make sure their efforts and results are communicated to senior people. Be positive about their achievements; if you don't and, instead, you complain about them, think what that says about you as team leader. If you're loyal to them, they'll be loyal to you.

- **Communicate**
  We mentioned feedback earlier in the context of the development of individuals, but it should be part of everything the team does. Review work frequently and let the team know how things are progressing. Make sure, too, that feedback works both ways – both from you on overall progress and back from them on how they, and you, are doing. They're the only ones that can tell you honestly what you're doing right (and wrong) as leader, so listen to them and act accordingly. And, when the job's done, don't forget to thank them for their contributions.

Project management

In a way, managing a project is the same as being a team leader, only bigger. Even if the project itself is small, managing it is a major responsibility. There's a specific task, or set of tasks, to be completed by a given deadline, within a certain budget and perhaps using particular resources. As project manager, it's up to you to make sure all these conditions are fulfilled. So, it's an important responsibility and an occasion for you to impress. Let's look at the steps you need to go through to make a success of it.

Establish who has overall responsibility

The person responsible for the project is usually the one who provides the budget, so right at the start you should organise a meeting with him to make sure you agree on the aim of the project and the areas of responsibility. Do this well in advance of the starting date because this is too important to rush. You'll have to agree on who else will need to be involved in the project and who has a vested interest in the outcome – otherwise known, in today's jargon, as the stakeholders.

After everything has been agreed, try to meet everyone involved individually and, if possible, as a group, so that they all know what you're trying to achieve. It's possible that some interests may want to put a different emphasis on certain things and it's easier to sort out conflicts before you start than when the project's up and running and demanding your full concentration.

brilliant tip

Be prepared to defend your decisions to your sponsor. Don't just agree with him if you think there's a better way to do things. Your firmness may annoy him at the time but, when it's clear that your decision was right, he'll appreciate it.

Write it all down

It's essential for you to have a clear idea of what you're trying to achieve from the start. If you know the destination, it's easier to plan your route. By writing out your objective, you'll force yourself to see if you completely understand it as well as the overall point of the project. If you're not sure, you won't be able to write it down and you'll know you need to ask some more questions.

By way of double-checking that you've understood the project's objective correctly, draft a document with the scope of the work on it and email it to your sponsor. Ask him to check that it coincides with his thinking on what the outcome should be. It's useful to have this in writing.

Engage the stakeholders

Use the meetings you have with them to get them on your side. Find out what they expect the project to achieve and how they'll measure its success. Stir up their enthusiasm for it and get them to agree to help where they can.

Create your plan

The more detailed your planning is, the fewer surprises you'll come across as work progresses. This is a form of brainstorming; don't worry about neatness, spelling, grammar or any of those things. Write down what has to be done to reach your objective. Make yourself focus on what needs to be achieved rather than how you'll achieve it. In other words, concentrate on results rather than activities.

Once you've jotted down everything that needs to be done, start rationalising it by identifying group work that can be done together, putting individual tasks into a practical, convenient sequence, checking to see if there are tasks that can be done in parallel. Decide on which tasks should have priority and set up milestones in the form of smaller goals that you need to achieve.

There are usually three sorts of problems which affect a project: it takes longer than it should, it costs more than it should or the quality of the work suffers because it has to be rushed or it's underfunded. You need to decide what elements of your project mustn't be compromised in terms of time, cost or quality.

Ask yourself where and what the risks are, how likely it is that they'll occur, how you'd deal with them if they did, and how much they'd cost you. The unfortunate fact is that, no matter how hard you work, there'll always be surprises and that's why you need to build contingency into your plan. The usual figure is about 15 per cent of the total budget.

brilliant tip

Your plan must include details of how long the project will take, how much work is involved and how much it'll cost. In other words, an estimate of the time, resources and budget.

Send the plan to your sponsor for approval and be prepared to have to negotiate. If he wants it sooner, you'll need to get more resources from him; if he wants to cut the budget, you'll have to point out that you won't be able to do as much work as you'd planned. When you reach a final agreement, get written approval for the version of the plan you'll be working from, just to make sure there are no 'misunderstandings' later.

Delegate and monitor the work

On the basis of the team's skills and capabilities, assign the various aspects of the work to individuals and groups, making sure that everyone understands and agrees to their responsibilities. Once work's under way, keep an eye on how everyone is progressing. Don't assume that, just because people know what they have to do, they actually do it. That's not being cynical; it's realistic.

Have regular meetings to monitor status. Keep them short and don't let people ramble on about what they've been up to; just ask them how far they've got and compare it with how far they're supposed to have got. If you've established a good, honest relationship with them, they'll be honest about where they are in their work and let you know about delays as soon as they happen. Get realistic estimates of how much longer they're likely to take. And, after the meeting, email the next steps to them, giving details of who's involved in every action and by when they need to be completed.

Watch your priorities

Keep a constant check on what you're trying to do and whether that's still what everyone wants. Things change all the time and you need to stay alert so that you can adapt as necessary. Complacency is lethal; stay nervous about it all, insecure even. Your job is to manage expectations right through the project, not just as you're getting near the deadline. At any point, if you're asked about the project, you should be in a position to reply confidently, give its current status and take no longer than 5 minutes to do so. You need to be in control all the time.

In fact, a weekly status report is useful for keeping your sponsor and stakeholders informed of the project's progress. It doesn't need to go into great details. Simply say whether:

- you're on course to meet the objective and, if not, what will be achieved and whether it will satisfy his needs;
- it's on time and, if not, how much longer it'll take;
- it's over, under or on budget.

A simple way of showing how each aspect of the work is progressing is to use a traffic lights symbol: Green = completed; Amber = under way/issues; Red = not yet started.

Team leader and project manager are both important jobs which carry a lot of responsibility. They'll test your knowledge of the tasks and the people involved, but they're challenges from which you'll learn a lot.

brilliant recap

- The basic elements of teamwork and the sorts of roles played by different team members.
- A detailed look at the role and responsibilities of the team leader.
- How to prepare and perform as a project manager.

CHAPTER 15

Strategies for success

f you want to succeed in the workplace, you need to be able to weigh up options and have the confidence to make decisions. Some will be about trivial things; others will be more complex and involve other people. Whatever the issue you're dealing with, try to keep it as simple as possible. Look at the bigger picture and don't get caught up in the nitty-gritty unless it's absolutely necessary. Too much information can be confusing, so just focus on things that'll have a direct influence on the end result. Most of all, get your working relationships right.

Getting on with others

The most important elements in any work situation are the people involved, so always try to see things from their point of view as well as your own. Work out who's likely be affected by your project, how they might react to it, and talk to them all individually to get their support. It'll make life easier for everyone, including you.

When you're in charge

If you're leading a team, treat team members with respect and, even if you start feeling stressed, make sure you don't take it out on them. They'll probably be working hard and may be feeling stressed themselves, so don't add to it. Keep the atmosphere positive and let them see you're ready to do any of the things necessary for getting the job done. On the other hand, your main energies should go towards managing the team, not doing things they could handle themselves. Be ready to delegate at an early stage so that you give everyone the time they need to do the job.

Don't hesitate to check how others have managed projects before. You can learn lots from their experiences, especially if you can isolate the ways of working that led to their success. Anticipate the sorts of obstacles you may have to face and work out how to overcome them. It also pays to imagine what impact your project will have when it's successfully completed. Once again, it's the power of positive thinking.

Don't wait until the end to do a post-mortem. You should be learning lessons all through the project. Use the weekly status meeting to share opinions on how things are progressing and make sure that everyone knows the importance of communicating what they learn. If you find that a chosen strategy isn't working, change tack, be flexible; there are many different ways of achieving your goal.

Decision time

How you reach your conclusions and make your decisions will depend on your own personality, but there are strategies you can use to streamline the process. It's not just a question of 'Here's the problem. What's the answer?' It can be broken down into more basic elements.

What's it all about?

This may seem pretty fundamental, but make sure first that you know exactly what the decision is about and by when you need to make it. Ask yourself why you need to make it, who else ought to be involved, and whether it depends on other decisions that haven't yet been made.

If it's definitely up to you, give yourself some thinking time – up to maybe an hour or so – to work out what information you have and what else you need to help you make an informed decision. Look for material that's reliable and easy to find.

 **tip**

Don't procrastinate. If you don't think you have enough information, don't use that as an excuse. When a decision's needed, it's better to make it on partial knowledge than not make it at all.

Increase your options

Don't be afraid to sound out others for their opinions, but be selective in who you consult. You obviously can't speak to everyone but you want to aim for a spread of opinions so that your focus isn't too narrow. Speak to people who'll be affected by what you decide – their input and support will help you to choose a course of action that'll be successful.

Your boss will want to know what's going on and be involved, so discuss it with him – even if it's only a brief progress report. There are other senior people who have the power to help get things done, too. Talking with them will move the project along more quickly, and they'll also appreciate the fact that you consulted them.

The more choices you develop, the better the decision you can make, so use all these discussions to help you to come up with as many options as possible. Try to get at least three; this avoids being stuck with a thankless either/or situation. List the choices and, with each one, weigh up the pros and cons and try to anticipate their likely outcomes. The aim is to identify the one which is the most practical and least risky. But theory and practice don't always coincide and there's an element of risk in nearly every decision anyway so, however difficult it is, make your choice.

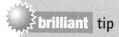 **tip**

Don't rely on flashes of inspiration or hunches which suggest a quick solution. Gather the information, use it to create as many options as possible and then consider them all systematically.

Follow it through

If you know there are people who'll be affected by what you've decided, make a point of telling them about it and try to get them on board. Making personal contact with them in that way will let them know they matter and help to keep them motivated. If you don't, and they hear it through the grapevine, it may have a negative effect on them.

Finally, it's your decision and you'll have to accept the consequences, so, when you've done all that, make sure it's implemented properly, that everyone who should contribute does so, and that you keep a check on its outcomes.

Deciding as a team

As we've seen, when making a decision on your own, there are lots of things to take into account; when the decision has to be made by a team, the potential complications multiply. There may be political manoeuvring, clashes of egos, friction between different interests, and discussions may turn into arguments. If this happens and you're the leader, concentrate on trying to resolve the issues and enabling the others to make some progress.

But whether you're in charge or not, you should do your best to get everyone involved. No one should be allowed to dominate discussions and everyone should have their say. Power struggles or inter-departmental squabbles lead to the notion that there are winners and losers in the debate – there aren't. The team has a common purpose. Be objective yourself and try to get others to follow suit. Listen to arguments from all sides and try to agree on the best answer, wherever it comes from. The whole process should be based on how good the ideas are, not on whether they're expressed by a friend or an enemy.

And, if you can't reach agreement on a particular issue, move on to something else and come back to it later. In the end, it may be up to the team leader to make the decision or you may choose to vote on it.

 **tip**

Don't argue against decisions unless you've got a very good reason to do so. If all you're doing is trying to score a point, it's not a constructive contribution. On the other hand, if your point is good and useful, don't give up on it just to avoid conflict.

Dealing with problems

Problems arise even in teams where everyone is friendly and cooperative. When they do, the first step is to acknowledge that they exist, then decide what's to be done about them. Don't let things such as embarrassment about raising an issue with someone get in the way; just be careful how you do it. Use the journalists' questions again.

Ask yourself:

- **Who ...** you should approach. First of all, it should be the person who's causing the problem. Try to sort things out with him, then allow some time to see if things improve. If they don't, you should talk with the group leader or manager. If she can't solve it and it's affecting the whole team, it's maybe time to call in an outsider, someone with the skills and objectivity to bring a fresh perspective to it.

- **Why ...** you should raise the issue and what you're trying to achieve by doing so. You need to be in a position to explain your reasons clearly to the person who's causing the problem.

- **When ...** you should raise it. Don't do it when tempers are frayed and emotions are running high, but don't let too long pass before you bring it up.

- **Where ...** you should raise it. Never criticise someone in front of everyone else or in any public place. Find a quiet spot where you can chat together without anyone overhearing you.

- **How ...** you should raise it. Give it some thought before you make any approach. Look at the facts and, if necessary, jot them down on paper. Think about how the person may react and work out how to deliver your message in a way that won't trigger any resentment in him. Say what you think is wrong and how he could do things differently, but don't be over-critical; be sensitive and try to get a balance between the negative and positive feedback you're giving him.

brilliant tip

Show your commitment to the project and try to make sure you keep the others motivated and enthusiastic too. Positive, cooperative attitudes are the key to success.

Problem – Lack of direction or focus

If you're team leader:

- Get everyone together and explain their individual roles and responsibilities. Make sure they know what they have to do and monitor progress on a weekly basis.

If you're a team member:

● Tell the team leader about your concerns and ask her to get the team together for a meeting and remind everyone of the team's goals and deadlines. Everyone should be clear on what they're supposed to be doing, what their deadlines are and who they should report to.

Problem – Lack of productivity
If you're team leader:

● Make sure someone's responsible for every piece of work and that all the others know who that person is. Everyone should be clear about the team's overall goal and deadlines and how their individual tasks are contributing to reaching that goal in time.

● Keep a regular check on progress. If work hasn't been done, find out why, but don't be critical. It's up to you to see that they're happy with their work and, if you need to make changes about speeding things up or asking for more effort, don't just impose them, but discuss them with those involved.

● Be honest and encourage team members to be the same. Recognise their achievements and thank them for doing a good job. If some don't reach their targets, don't criticise them; ask them how or why it happened and work with them to find a way to avoid it happening again in the future.

If you're a team member:

● Know your deadlines and try hard to meet them. If you're unhappy about something or don't feel motivated, discuss it with your team leader and work with her to try to find ways of making the job more satisfying.

Problem – Personality clashes

If you're team leader:

- First, speak to the people concerned separately. Try to understand why they don't get on and what's causing the friction. Then speak to them together, ask what they intend to do about the problem, and be ready to make some suggestions of your own. Be careful not to seem to be taking sides.

- Keep an eye on things to see whether that's made a difference and, after a few weeks, have more meetings with them, separately and together.

- Of course, it'll also help if you can arrange for them to work in completely different areas and have as little contact as possible.

If you're a team member:

- Try to be positive and respect others' points of view even if they are very different from your own. If you can, see past their differences and look for something you like about them or some things on which you do agree.

- Don't let bad feelings just keep on simmering. Bring up the issue sooner rather than later. Talk to the person involved in private and ask if he has problems with you. If his attitude is causing you stress, say so. Don't try to force him to understand your ideas on the job – let him know you'd rather the two of you made the effort – even if it's only to agree to disagree.

- If that's difficult or impossible, talk to your team leader and let her know what's going on. Don't be critical of the other person; just say you're not getting on with him and you'd rather work in a different area if that's possible.

Problem – Internal bullying

If you're team leader:

- Make sure everyone knows, right up front, that you won't tolerate it and that, if it does happen, the victim can come and tell you about it in confidence and you'll do what's needed to put a stop to it.

If you're a team member:

- Don't pretend it's not happening. Make a note of what happened, with dates and times. If it's affecting your health, get a letter from your doctor or a psychiatrist.

- Try to be more assertive. Stay calm and reasonable and tell the person responsible that his behaviour's unacceptable. Tell him exactly what he did that upset you and how it made you feel. If it's not possible to do that, or if he doesn't take it seriously, talk to your team leader or mentor.

Problem – The group's too friendly and not critical enough of their work

If you're team leader:

- Don't deflate the group but let them know they're maybe not as good as they think they are. Create an atmosphere which encourages them to want to keep on improving and which welcomes and rewards constructive feedback.

If you're a team member:

- Don't just go with the flow and accept everyone's ideas uncritically – think about them, discuss and even challenge them, and get others to comment on your own ideas.

Problem – The group becomes a sort of exclusive club

If you're team leader:

- Change the nature of the team by including people who haven't been part of it before.

- Make each member of your team responsible for maintaining contacts and interchanges of opinions with an external group not otherwise connected with their own.

If you're a team member:

- Make sure you meet people outside the team (but inside the company). Talk about the project with them and get their opinions on it. Let your own team members know you're doing that and try to get them to do the same.

Problem – Working in a virtual team across geographical boundaries

If you're team leader:

- Wherever they are, the team members all have the same purpose and goal. Part of your job is to make sure they all understand that. The fact that they live and work in different places and only communicate via emails, phones or teleconferences is irrelevant – a virtual team is still a team.

If you're a team member:

- Face-to-face contacts will be limited or perhaps non-existent, so use all the computing and telecommunications technology that's available to communicate frequently with team members who aren't in your part of the world.

Cross-cultural teams

At some point, you may well find yourself working in a multicultural team. We're not listing this as a problem but it's likely to be a very different experience from working in a team of people who all have more or less the same background.

Different cultures have different attitudes to things. In fact, teams with a cultural mix are often more effective, since they're drawing on the best of the varied approaches the different team members bring to a challenge. It also gives you the opportunity to broaden your own perceptions and knowledge.

Respect the differences

We take our own culture for granted and it's easy to assume that everyone shares the same values. That's an unsophisticated stance and it can lead to misunderstandings. We need to be sensitive to potential differences in terms of the importance of and attitudes to:

- the individual;
- religion;
- age, gender, background, status and position;
- appearance.

We also need to recognise that others may place different stress on:

- punctuality and time;
- following rules and regulations;
- respect for hierarchy; and
- being empowered to take individual responsibility.

Attitudes to work may vary considerably. The pace of life may be faster or slower and so work hours and breaks may vary considerably from yours. Work may be a crucial part of, or a sort of intrusion into, a person's overall lifestyle. And there may be a suspicion, dislike or even a fear of 'foreigners'.

When it comes to making decisions, you may find conflicting tendencies. Negotiations may seem adversarial and compromise can appear to be a sign of weakness. Some will be rational in their approach, others intuitive, and conclusions may be reached by arriving at a consensus or simply by accepting to do as someone directs.

Even the apparently simple business of communicating can have hidden traps. Overly friendly approaches may be discouraged, along with directness or bluntness, which may seem impolite. Some may prefer more formal contacts, avoiding colloquial speech and using titles and surnames rather than first names, but others may welcome a more relaxed style. And when we get to issues of body language, eye contact, touching and the possible invasion of personal space, variations can be extreme. But however strange some of these customs may seem to you, remember that yours will be as strange to them. The important thing to remember is that mutual respect for differences will help everyone to work and succeed together.

brilliant recap

- The importance of having respect for others.
- Leading a team.
- Tips on decision making.
- Some potential problems arising from working in a team and how to solve them.
- The importance of understanding and respecting cultural differences.

CHAPTER 16

You and your boss

The language of organisations still reflects their hierarchical nature. You frequently hear or read of things going 'all the way up' to senior management or 'all the way down' to cleaners. Of course, levels of responsibility vary enormously, but then so do the rewards that go with them. When it comes to your relationship with your boss, it's better for both of you if, rather than think in terms of him being a master and you being a servant, you have a healthy, two-way partnership. OK, he's the boss, but you're not powerless – he relies on you. If you don't deliver, he can't do his job properly – and vice versa. So you need to be aware of how he likes to work and what you can do to keep him happy and make your own way 'up' through the ranks.

A balanced working relationship

There's no point just hoping that you and your boss are going to get on well together. Your own progress depends on the two of you developing a good relationship based on mutual understanding and respect. He'll expect certain things from you and you have the right to expect support and encouragement from him. In other words, in some ways, each of you is managing the other. So, right from the start, try to get a clear idea of what he expects, what his own strengths and weaknesses are, how he reacts to pressure, how he prefers to work, and what goals and objectives are important to him.

If he doesn't set up a meeting for the first week of your job, take the initiative yourself and ask if you can get together to discuss things before you start. That way, you can find out:

- what he expects from you;
- what your responsibilities are;
- how much freedom you have to take the initiative;
- what resources are available to you;
- his preferred method of communication, his views on working early and late, and whether he's content to see results or also wants to know how you achieved them.

Also, since this, remember, is a two-way process, you can take the opportunity to tell him what your expectations are, the sorts of skills you'd like to develop, the way you like to work and the resources you'll need to do the job properly.

brilliant tip

Before you even start work, you may have an idea of what you expect bosses to be like or the idea may be shaped by how your first boss treats you. But, like everyone else, they vary considerably. It's important to approach each new one with an open mind. Never assume that he's going to be like the old one was.

It works both ways

If the relationship is genuinely two-way, it means that you have control of your part of it. If you manage that properly, it'll make his job easier and reflect well on you. So, do the best job you can, produce high-quality work, and always get to meetings on time and fully prepared for anything that may arise. If you can think of ways of improving things, take the initiative and make the changes. But keep him informed of what you're doing with brief, regular reports, using his preferred method of communication. Remember that his performance is being measured as well as yours, so find out how you can help him meet his targets.

To establish the required balance, find out the sorts of things that impress him, the sorts of attitudes he admires, and try to use that knowledge in your dealings with him. Get to know his weaknesses and try to make them your strengths, and work in a way which complements what he's doing. That doesn't mean you're losing your individuality; it increases your sensitivity to people and helps you to develop skills that'll be useful in broader negotiations.

If the relationship sometimes feels strained, remember he has things on his mind which don't relate to you. Resist the temptation to moan about him in public. In fact, loyalty is very important. However 'justified' you think your criticism of him may be, keep it to yourself. In fact, you should defend him and stress his good points if others are being critical. Never contradict him in public; wait until it's just the two of you and make your point then. If you think he's done a good job on a project, say so. It's not being sycophantic; it's all helping to foster a good working relationship based on mutual trust and respect.

brilliant tip

You need to micro-manage his expectations of you. Don't promise things you may not be able to deliver. If you have a problem, tell him about it right away. And if you make a mistake, make sure he hears it from you before somebody else tells him about it.

Boss types

As we said, all bosses are different but, when it comes to how they work themselves and how they manage their staff, most of them fall into an identifiable category by tending to lean towards one end of the spectrum rather than the other. If that's the case with yours, accept his style and adapt your own so that it's easier to work with him.

The information spectrum

 **examples**

- **Paula** is obsessed with detail. She's very thorough and scrutinises everything very carefully to make sure she knows all the details and background context. With her, you need to know your facts and your sources, communicate clearly and logically, and make sure you can support your work with the relevant data and information.

- **Jessica**, on the other hand, prefers the 'Big Picture'. She's less concerned with details and feels more comfortable with a broader overview of your work. With her, your best strategy is to avoid dwelling on background material and instead offer general summaries of what you're doing and report outcomes and objectives.

The problems spectrum

brilliant **examples**

- **Dennis** is basically a bureaucrat. He sticks to the rules and regulations, likes to know exactly what's going on and keeps a note of everything. So, give him plenty of time and space to make decisions. Put everything you want to communicate to him in writing and always keep a copy yourself. And if you think changes are needed, suggest them gradually and always make sure you can back them up by quoting company policy.

- **George**, on the other hand, likes change. He's active, dynamic and always on the lookout for new and better ways of doing things. So, if his ideas are good, be enthusiastic about them and get involved in implementing them. Be creative yourself, suggest improvements, propose new approaches to procedures, share your ideas.

The work spectrum

 **examples**

- In a way, **Celia** is chaotic. She's forgetful, has no sense of time passing and has so many jobs going at the same time that she can't really focus properly on any of them. With her, you need to be organised. You'll probably end up having to sort things out for her, so make sure you know where everything is and what's going on. When you suggest or ask for something, follow it up if you think she's forgotten about it. And always be ready to prompt her at meetings and anticipate what she needs.

- **Kate**'s at the other end of the scale. She's highly organised and tends to focus on one task at a time. Logic and order are what please her and she always knows exactly what needs to be done, by whom and by when. So you, too, need to be organised, punctual and stick to schedules. It's a question here of mirroring the way she works.

The management spectrum

 **examples**

- No two ways about it, **Frank** is a control freak. He always needs to know what you're doing and wants to be involved in everything to make sure it's being done his way and to his standards. It's easy to annoy someone like this, so get his trust by doing the work exactly as he specified it should be done and keeping him updated with your progress before he even asks you to. Once you've got his respect this way, you can carefully introduce other ways of doing things if need be.

- Frank would never be able to work with **Jack**. He's laid back and a sort of 'hands off' boss. You'll rarely see Jack interfering with what you're doing – he just expects you to get on with it. So that's what you should do. Keep him informed but don't bother talking about the trivial stuff. Make it obvious that he can trust you.

Points of conflict

All relationships have their good and bad moments, and sometimes they don't work at all. If you find you don't like your boss, or vice versa, don't let that get in the way. You don't have to like each other, but you're working together so you need to respect each other and cooperate to get the job done. If things are interfering with that, try to meet and discuss the problems.

First of all, though, be sure that it's worth it. If it's something you can put up with and the project's going well, don't risk that for a trifle. Have a private meeting and give your boss a chance to sort it all out.

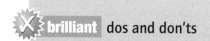 **dos and don'ts**

Do

✔ Try to give a balanced view. Say what works as well as what doesn't

✔ Be honest about how you'd like to be treated

✔ Keep an open mind and try to see his point of view

✔ Focus on finding a solution rather than dwelling on the problem

✔ Summarise the decisions you've made to make sure you're agreed on them

Don't

✘ Complain unless you can suggest a solution

✘ Be aggressive. The idea is to find a solution, not just assign blame

✘ Use what other people have said to attack your boss

✘ Be smug if he admits he's made a mistake

If, despite all your efforts, the problems persist, you may need to contact Human Resources about moving teams, departments or, if the worst comes to the worst, even leaving the job. But that's definitely a last resort. If you're lucky, you'll have a boss who appreciates and rewards you; if you're not, it's up to you to make your case.

Problem – Too big a workload

In this instance, the first thing to do is make sure you both understand exactly what you're supposed to be doing. You'll often find, when you ask for clarification, that things haven't been thought through properly, so don't waste time working until your boss knows what she wants. You could help her to prioritise your work into the 'Must do', 'Should do' and 'Would be nice to do if there was time' categories.

If you keep a record of the hours you've worked, you can use that to show that you don't mind the occasional heavy workload, but that it shouldn't be the norm. You have to learn to say 'no'. Keep it polite, but be ready to explain why you can't do the extra that's being asked. You could even suggest other ways in which the task could be done. If you're consistent, others will know that you'll help when you can but that 'no' means 'no'. If you say 'yes' all the time, it won't necessarily raise your profile – on the contrary, you might get a reputation for being an easy touch. On top of that, work will be more stressful.

So, if your boss asks you to do something, ask yourself these questions:

- Is it part of my job?
- What's in it for me in terms of learning or experience?
- When's it got to be done?
- Can it be done by someone else?

● If I say 'yes', how will it affect my present workload? Will I need to stay late or work at weekends?

● What'll happen if I say 'no'? Will it affect my career or promotion prospects?

Problem – Promotion or pay rise

It's important to be realistic about your performance. If you're confident you can justify your request, arrange a meeting. Be diplomatic and reasonable rather than demanding. Explain why you think you deserve a rise. Give details of particular jobs you've done which suggest you're worth it. If you know of jobs similar to your own for which people are getting paid more, use them as evidence.

It may be that there are factors which put obstacles in the way. If so, learn to deal with them. It may be that your boss depends on you a lot and, if you're promoted, she'd lose you. If that's the case, say you'll help to train whoever replaces you. If she doesn't have the authority to make the decision, try to get her help to make your case with the person who does.

Of course, the obstacles might be harder than that. She might not believe you should get the rise or promotion. If that's the case, work out why she feels that way and what you need to do in order to change her mind. Or she may not give you credit and pretend instead that your ideas are hers. Keeping records to prove they're your ideas will help you overcome that one. And if the difficulties persist, discuss the problem with your mentor, or a Human Resources rep.

Problem – Holidays

This shouldn't really be difficult. Make sure you book the dates well in advance and confirm them in writing – by email, for example – to avoid misunderstandings. Then, as it gets nearer to the time, remind your boss that you'll be away.

Make it easy for workmates by arranging for someone to take care of any issues that arise while you're gone. Think of the possible problems that could crop up and plan for them. And give yourself plenty of time to tidy things up before you leave.

> **brilliant tip**
>
> The question of training should never be a problem. You simply need to remind the people concerned that developing your skills and getting some extra coaching will make you even more efficient and effective.

Problem – Responsibility

This is where you need to get the balance right and be realistic about how much you can cope with. If you want more responsibility, don't try to get it by moaning that you're not being challenged. Point to specific pieces of work that you could do; suggest work-shadowing your boss or a more experienced colleague. But, if you do take on extra responsibility, make sure you still do your own job properly.

If you think too much is being asked of you, make a list of all your responsibilities and how much time you spend on each one. Go through it with your boss, identify the ones you want to keep and suggest who might be able and willing to take on the others.

Problem – Sexual harassment

This can lead to real distress whether it's blatant and direct or suggestive and indirect and it takes many forms, including:

- touching or brushing against a colleague inappropriately;
- making remarks about someone's appearance in a sexual context;

- commenting on someone's sex life or sexual performance – real or imagined;
- suggesting benefits for sexual favours;
- making obvious sexual advances;
- forcing yourself sexually on someone.

Don't hesitate to let the person know that you find their behaviour offensive. If that doesn't stop them, find out whether the company has a sexual harassment policy – nowadays, most do – and follow the set procedures. Be systematic about it: keep a note of how you followed the procedures and what the outcome was. Even if there isn't a set company procedure, don't be put off making a complaint. In order to make sure it's not just one person's word against another, collect all available evidence, get witnesses and find out if there are others who've been victimised too.

You need to document:

- Who did it.
- What they did.
- What provoked it.
- When it happened.
- Where it happened.
- If there were any witnesses.
- How it made you feel.

Problem – Bullying

First, try to resolve it by speaking to the person who's bullying you. Tell him his behaviour's unacceptable. Be calm but certainly not submissive as you're talking. Stand up straight, look him in the eye and speak with authority. You know you're in the right here. Give him specific examples – as many as you can, and certainly more than one – of how he's offended you and why you're not going to tolerate it.

If that doesn't stop him, make an official complaint. Make a note of when the bullying takes place and how it makes you feel, and speak to your mentor, a Human Resources rep or a senior manager you know you can trust.

Problems with your boss

Despite your best efforts, you may find that you and your boss just don't get on and that it affects the way you work. If that's the case, you might feel you need to take it to a higher authority such as a senior manager, your mentor or someone in Human Resources. It's a big step, so make sure you're ready for it.

- Don't make it personal. Resist the temptation to say how horrible your boss is and focus instead on how things need to change.

- Keep a diary and list in detail what the issues are, when they happened, the effect they have on you and what you've done to try to resolve them.

- Your boss will obviously be annoyed if you bring this up with a higher authority and he has to explain his actions. He may ask to meet you to discuss it. If he does, stay calm and be ready to defend your position. Listen to his side of the story and don't forget that you're trying to solve a problem, not assign blame. But don't let him bully you; don't submit to him. You've taken this big step so don't give in; make sure things get sorted out.

Your basic rights are clear:

- You should be fairly rewarded (in terms of pay, promotion, training and growth opportunities) for the work you do, irrespective of your sex, colour, religion or age.

- You should be allowed to enjoy a life outside work.

- You should not have to work under threat, abuse or any condition that affects your mental or physical well-being.

- You should not have to do anything with which you are morally uncomfortable.

The annual appraisal

Most companies have an annual appraisal where you meet with your boss or mentor to look at how you've performed over the previous year, discuss training needs and possible promotion. If you and your boss get on well and communicate regularly, it should be a straightforward session. The first time, though, it can feel strange and you may feel a bit vulnerable. But it's not just a one-way process: you're being assessed but it also gives you the chance to bring up any points you want to mention.

Be prepared

Before the meeting comes around, make a list of the work you've done during the year, what you've achieved, and note any areas outside your present remit where you've contributed to the organisation. Your notes should also include any significant work-related issues you'd like to discuss and some feedback on your boss. It's not always asked for, but it helps to have something to say, just in case.

Think about the year to come as well. Spell out your objectives, list the skills you'd like to develop and the roles you'd like to fill, and investigate the promotion opportunities and salary increases that may come along. Find out what the company's promotion criteria are and check them to see how you measure up.

If you're asked to book a room for the meeting, find one that's suitable for a confidential conversation and where you won't be disturbed. Book it for twice as long as you think you'll need because you don't want to have to rush through things. And make sure you get there on time and ready for anything.

Taking feedback

Feedback's intended to help you, so look for practical suggestions and specific examples of what you could do to improve. Stay objective and listen carefully. If you let personal feelings intrude, you may miss some valuable advice. The appraisal and criticism of where and how you need to improve isn't an attack on you personally, especially if the criticism's constructive.

On the other hand, don't take too much notice if it's purely destructive; that has only negative effects. If you think some of the things that are said are unfair, don't be afraid to say so.

brilliant tip

Boasting is obviously not a good strategy. On the other hand, don't be overly modest. If you're complimented on your work during the appraisal, don't be embarrassed about it; accept it with grace.

Giving feedback

If you're asked for feedback and you haven't prepared for that, ask if you could give the issues some thought and fix on a date and time to have another meeting. When you do give feedback, keep your remarks constructive. Don't make any personal attacks; focus instead on the nature of the problem. And don't bring up any problem unless you can think of a solution for it. Finally, don't be vague; be specific.

brilliant recap

- The importance of establishing a balanced, two-way relationship with your boss.
- The different types of boss you may encounter.
- Potential points of conflict and how to deal with them.
- The annual appraisal and giving and taking feedback.

CHAPTER 17

You and your customers

f your first thought on seeing this chapter heading was: 'Not relevant. I don't deal with external clients so I don't have any customers', you're mistaken. Anyone who relies on you to provide services, products, information or anything else that helps them to do their job is your customer. They may be colleagues, but they're still your customers and they expect to be treated well. Here, we'll look at the basics of how to make your interaction with customers positive and rewarding for you and them.

Not always right, but always important

No, the customer isn't always right – they make mistakes like everyone else. But they do have certain expectations of you in the way of service and it's in your interest to try to satisfy them. If you don't take care of them the way they want you to, they'll go and find someone else who will. As with other things, there's no golden rule about how to succeed, because each client is different and you'll never get to know them all completely, so don't make any assumptions, but do try to base your dealings with them on some common-sense principles.

Make them your priority

If you treat them as the most important part of the job you're doing, they'll feel valued and important. Don't think of them as interrupting your 'real job'; they're fundamental to why you're there at all. Try to see things from their viewpoint, understand how they feel and make yourself available for them. They want attention and recognition, so find out how they prefer to communicate – email, phone, face to face – give them your contact details and make it easy for them to get in touch. Make sure your voicemail and email systems are working well so that you receive all the messages they send. And always return their calls as soon as possible.

brilliant tip

They'll be at their most anxious for your help when there's a problem. The natural tendency is to hope the problem will go away. It probably won't and that's not what the customer wants anyway, so don't ignore it. Get in touch with them and do what you can to try to solve it. If you try to avoid it, they won't be getting in touch again soon.

Mutual understanding

Lots of problems occur as a result of poor communications and the consequent misunderstandings. Whenever you're discussing issues, make sure you both understand them in the same way and that you agree on what they are. You want to be sure you're on the same wavelength, so ask questions, summarise comments that are made, and don't be afraid to cover the same ground more than once.

If they ask you for something, get it or do it right away. If it's something that needs organising, give them a time scale and make sure you stick to it. If you say you're going to do it, they believe you and expect you to deliver. If you fail, they'll remember it. If whatever it is can't be done immediately, just tell them why and let them know when you'll do it. And don't make promises you can't keep or say things you don't believe yourself. That's the quickest way to kill a relationship.

Show a positive attitude

Don't start by seeing all the difficulties involved or thinking about things you can't do. Make your first impulse positive and identify the things you can do to help. You want to give the impression of competence, a 'Yes we can' approach. This doesn't mean pretending the negatives aren't there or agreeing with everything the customer says; it means managing expectations from a positive, confident perspective.

brilliant dos and don'ts

Do

✔ Admit it when you don't have an answer, but say that you'll find out about it

✔ Be ready to redirect queries to others who can help

✔ Be sympathetic when a customer is feeling frustrated or helpless.

✔ Apologise if things go wrong

✔ Reassure customers that you'll deal with them as quickly as you can or that you'll call them back

Don't

✘ Just say 'I don't know' when you're asked something

✘ Make excuses such as 'I'm not allowed to do that' or 'That's not my job'

✘ Dodge responsibility or blame someone else for things that go wrong

✘ Patronise customers

✘ Ever imply that they're being unreasonable (even when they are)

✘ Say you're too busy to deal with them and they should call you back

If you can anticipate developments and sort things out before they become problems, your stock will rise. You want people to be happy with your service, so try to treat them even better than they expect. It helps if you get to know them personally, know what sorts of things they like and what turns them off. Treat them well, show an interest in them, smile when you meet them. And, even when it's just a phone conversation, be upbeat – your attitude will come across in your voice. Suggestions such as this may sound corny (or perhaps even obvious) but, in the end, if you make the experience of dealing with you personal and enjoyable, they're more likely to stay with you.

brilliant tip

Judge how formal or informal your relationship with your client should be with care. If you're at the same level, informality's easier and you could, for example, use first names. But if she's more senior than you, take your cue from her.

Be professional

No matter how friendly you become with a client, never share your problems with them – whether they're personal issues or connected to your company. You don't want to come across as a whinger or a gossip; people respect loyalty. If there's something about the company you don't like, talk to somebody internal about it, never to outsiders. In fact, you should be aware that, in all these dealings, you're representing the company – your attitudes and professionalism reflect on your employers. If there are problems, be sensitive and discreet about them. If you're asked direct questions about internal issues, remember that you're not obliged to give out any information; be polite and find a way round it. That's not being evasive; it's being loyal and professional, and you'll be respected for it.

 **tip**

Be prepared for anything. If you make sure you know what's going on in your own and your client's company, you won't be caught out when you're told something you should have known already.

When you've established a good relationship with a client, work at keeping it fresh. The tendency sometimes is to give someone special treatment when you're trying to get their business. If it works and, once you've hooked them, you show less interest in them, they'll notice it. So think about it – which is more valuable to you, a customer you already have or one you're trying to get?

Complaints

We've been encouraging you to be positive in everything and, perhaps surprisingly, we're now saying the same thing about complaints. They're often seen as being negative and there's no doubt that having someone yelling abuse at you about the awful service they've received is unpleasant and embarrassing. But complaints are part of good customer service; without complaints, you won't know what may be offending your customers and making them take their business elsewhere.

However good you may be, you can't possibly be perfect for everyone, so complaints go with the territory. If you approach them positively, you can turn their negative aspect to your advantage by sorting them out. Think about it. The client is angry, disappointed; you listen, understand, say how you're going to solve the problem and do so. The client is impressed, goes away happy and, perhaps most importantly, tells people how well you've handled it rather than badmouthing you.

The other point is that complaints highlight things you should know about how you're performing. If one person has been offended by something, it's probable that others have felt the same way, so it's best for it to be pointed out to you so that you can do something about it. So, while you don't want to encourage people to complain, you should let them know that you'd appreciate feedback on what they like and dislike about your service provision and any improvements they'd like to see. The important thing then is to act on what they say. If you don't, the process is useless and will just look like a PR stunt.

Most people don't like complaining, so make it easy for them by:

- asking for their opinions of the service;
- letting them know that complaints are welcome;
- giving them plenty of ways – by phone, in writing and in person – to give you feedback;
- being approachable – if they like you, they'll want to give you a second chance so they'll want to get problems sorted out;
- reacting positively to complaints by making changes.

Dealing with complaints

As we said at the start, the customer's not always right. On the other hand, they won't be your customer for long if you tell them so. The trick is to make the person who's complaining feel that he's made a valid point and that you've listened and you'll do something about it. Forget about who's to blame – that's not the issue; the priority is to solve the problem. You won't have to do much – even a small gesture will make him feel you're taking his point and acting on it.

Basically, he wants to know that you're listening to him. Quite often, complaining is born out of frustration; he wants an outlet for that by getting it all off his chest. Only when he's done that and calmed down a little is he ready to listen to possible solutions. So, let him have his say first, then, if it's appropriate, apologise, say you understand and offer an explanation and a solution. Don't be afraid to empathise with him; it doesn't mean you're admitting liability (which is an important consideration from a legal point of view). Let him know that you care about what he's saying.

If the ranting goes on too long and he's rude or hostile, end the conversation politely and offer to call him back. Stay calm and let him know that you and your company value his business but prefer it to be conducted in a businesslike way.

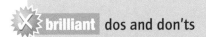 **dos and don'ts**

Do

✔ Listen to everything and say little; it's the customer's views that matter, not yours

✔ Stay calm and courteous even if the other person is rude or unpleasant

✔ Give him the benefit of the doubt and assume he's telling the truth

Don't

✘ Jump straight in with attempts to resolve the issue

✘ Justify your actions

✘ Argue

✘ Take any abuse, no matter how important the customer is (or thinks he is)

If you're the person who's listened to the complaint, it's your responsibility to see that it's dealt with, no matter whose fault it is. If you can't sort it out yourself, pass it to someone who can. Don't waste time dealing with people who don't have the power to solve it and don't pass the customer on to someone else. We all know how annoying it is to be passed from person to person as we wait for an answer.

brilliant tip

When people are angry they tend to speak loudly or even shout. It's natural to match your own level to theirs but you should try to resist this tendency. If you keep your voice and manner calm and controlled as you answer, the person complaining will begin to match your volume.

The process works best if you reach a solution together. Ask the customer how she thinks the problem might be solved, but remember she may ask for more than she expects to get, so don't just accept and agree with everything; try to get her to be more reasonable. If she doesn't have any ideas about how to resolve it, give her some choices. But don't try just pushing a solution on to her. If she's not happy with the outcome, the problem still hasn't gone away.

Try to sort things out as quickly as you can. The longer it takes, the more annoyed she'll get and the more she'll be inclined to complain to others, with the result that you and your company get a bad reputation. Once you've set solutions in motion, keep her informed of how they're progressing and, when the problem has been solved, go back to her after a week or two to check that she's happy with the outcome and the way you dealt with it all.

Get to know your client

It's all too easy to assume you know what your clients want and the longer you deal with particular issues, the more you think you know what's involved. But these assumptions aren't always based on real data and, quite often, they're wrong. The way to avoid them is to know all your customers as individuals so that you can be sure of what they really want. What you're doing then is customising the service you offer so that the customer knows he can trust you and so will be more likely to stay with you.

So, how do you find out what each individual wants? Easy – ask them. They may not know or, even if they do, they may find it difficult to translate it into practical terms, but starting a dialogue with them will provide you with data on which you can base your perceptions of them. It'll also give you an idea of who your best clients are and which ones are more trouble than they're worth.

brilliant questions

This series of questions will help you to assess clients and form a clear picture of how you relate to them.

First of all, as people:

(Q) How do they make their decisions?

(Q) Who has ultimate responsibility?

(Q) What kind of person are they? Do they like facts or do they work by intuition?

Next, their buying behaviour:

(Q) What do they buy and how often do they buy it?

(Q) Do they pay on time, or very late? Do they need reminding of the need to pay?

(Q) Do they demand a lot of after-sales service? How much does this cost you? Is the cost greater than the reward?

Finally, their value:

(Q) How valuable are they to you, now and in the future? If you lost them, how much revenue would you lose? Do you think they could produce more revenue in the future?

(Q) Why are they valuable to you? Is it because of the profits they generate, the credibility they bring to your business, or some other reason?

Entertaining

It's generally accepted that building good working relation-ships leads to success and one of the ways this is achieved is through entertaining clients at functions such as business lunches and dinners, drinks and hospitality events. Such things may sound glamorous but the glamour can be quite superficial. Nonetheless, they're part of the customer relations process, so if you're invited to corporate trips, sports events, concerts or whatever else, accept the invitation unless you have a good reason not to. If you find you're getting asked to so many events outside working hours that they're interfering with your private life, talk to your boss about it.

Make sure you find out the appropriate dress code and that your guest knows it as well. There aren't really any rules about topics of conversation but try to avoid talking about business if you can or keep it to a minimum. If the event involves drink, the usual reservations apply. By all means drink, unless you're driving, but keep it on the lowest possible side of moderate. Never mind what others are doing; you want to stay in control. Equally, you don't want your guests making fools of them-selves, so behave responsibly towards them and don't ply them with alcohol. If they do have a lot to drink, organise a taxi for them, but without making a fuss.

If you're the customer

The same advice we've given above applies equally to the cus-tomer. It's in both your interests to build a relationship. If you approach someone for help or services, he's more likely to oblige if you treat him as an ally rather than an enemy.

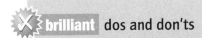 **brilliant** dos and don'ts

Do

✔ Be polite but firm, friendly but professional

✔ Expect (and demand) good service, without acting like a prima donna

✔ Stay calm as you express your feelings of disappointment and dissatisfaction

Don't

✗ Get aggressive with people. It only makes them defensive

✗ Shout at someone because you're dissatisfied with them; think of and suggest ways they might help you instead

Don't expect the person to know what you want. Before you talk to him, have a good idea of what's needed and how he might provide it. The clearer you are about what you want and the better you communicate it, the more likely you are to get it. So make sure he understands what you want and get his commitment, in writing, to get it for you. That's proof that he's accepted responsibility for delivering the service. Make sure he knows he has that responsibility by asking for his name. Apart from anything else, it means that you won't have to explain everything again the next time it crops up.

 recap

- Your relationship with customers of all sorts.
- Understanding customers' needs and taking a positive, professional approach to meeting them.
- The nature and value of complaints and how to deal with them.
- The importance of getting to know your client.
- How to survive corporate entertainment

CHAPTER 18

Managing
yourself

S uccess doesn't just depend on luck and you're not going to reach your potential if you sit back and hope someone else will do what's needed. You've got to make your own luck by being active and actually managing yourself and your career to make the most of what's on offer. From choosing the right career path to taking care of yourself so that you stay healthy and sane, you need to be the one in charge. It means really understanding who you are, what you're like, what's important to you and what you want to get out of life. These are the topics we'll be looking at in this chapter.

Planning your career

There's a big difference between a job and a career. If you focus on your day-to-day activities at work, you don't see the big picture – your career. And by the time you do get round to stepping back to see where you are, it may be too late to have the effect on it you'd like to. So don't let this happen to you. Set yourself a career plan, think it through, keep checking it against your progress, and use it to make things happen the way you want them to.

Your plan

A plan is most useful if it's reduced to significant bullet points rather than long aspirational paragraphs. After all, your goals or dreams may change, so you just need some guidelines so that, when you revisit the plan, it's easy to adapt it. With that in mind, we'd suggest you shape your plan around the answers you give to the questions below. Keep a note of the questions and your answers and revisit them now and then:

- Where are you now in terms of your role and responsibilities?
- Where do you want to be in five years' time?
- Who is currently in the position you'd like to occupy?
- Why do you want to be in that position? (This involves listing aspects of the job that appeal to you and helps you understand what's important to you. As time passes, your priorities will probably change, so this will help you to keep track of which things are still important and which are less so.)
- What do you need to do to be in that position? (Here, you need to think carefully and be specific. Think about the knowledge, skills and experience you need to do the job well.)
- How are you going to work towards being promoted to that post? (It might involve taking training courses in different skills, taking on specific responsibilities, even reading books and consulting relevant websites.)

Don't think of these goals as hard and fast rules. If you do, you'll be imprisoned by them. Success takes time and opportunities often come from surprising directions, so be flexible and patient and use them as guidelines.

brilliant tip

Don't be timid when you answer these questions and lay out your plans. Assume that just about everything is possible. Think big. The only thing that can hold you back is yourself.

Making the plan work

The first thing to do is find the right job. Don't just grab at anything that comes along; make sure you always have a reason for being in the position you've chosen. It should be one in which you can:

- develop the skill base and/or get the experience you need;
- follow a path that leads to the position you want;
- make important contacts;
- earn enough money to meet your needs.

If your job's not helping you to do at least one of these things, you should probably rethink your position.

Develop your skills

When you're just starting out, you have the scope and opportunities to experiment and learn new skills and it's important to grab every opportunity you have to do so. You may be tempted to stick with your strengths because that feels more secure, but step outside your comfort zone, identify your weak spots and improve or eliminate them. It may seem to make you less impressive an employee but, in the long run, it'll help you to acquire all-round skills that'll equip you to be more flexible and more responsive in much wider contexts. Stay curious; never stop learning. There'll come a time when you're doing a job which calls for you to focus mostly on the things you do best, but never give up the chance of picking up new skills and always make sure you keep updating your old ones.

Ask around

All companies have their own ways of doing things and the quickest way of finding out how yours operates is by asking others for advice or guidance on things. There are lots of people who can help you.

- You can discuss your position and aims with company mentors on a formal or informal basis.
- If you have a specific position in mind, try talking to someone who's already doing a similar job.
- Consult professional career advisers.
- And don't rule out colleagues and friends, who may know you well enough to have an idea of what sort of things you'd be good at – things you might not have thought of yourself.

Check promotion prospects

If your company has a set of guidelines for promotion, follow them. Do what's needed, make a note of your activities and use them to support your case when you're discussing promotion. Find out who'll be deciding whether you should be promoted or not and have a chat with them well before the promotion question arises. Ask them what you need to do to increase your chances; get them to be direct and specific, then work on any areas where you (or they) think you need to improve. In the end, you have to market yourself, but we'll deal with that later.

Personal development plan (PDP)

When you start out, the workplace can seem vast, alien, and full of bewildering options, with chances to widen and deepen your experience everywhere. Try everything. Don't be afraid to make mistakes – that's often the best way to learn. There are training courses on everything and plenty of things to learn, so, to keep things simple for you, break that comprehensive whole down into specific areas. It'll help you to focus on what you need to do in order to develop.

Knowledge
- **General**
  Watch the news, read the papers, keep up with what's going on, not just in your own region or country, but in the world.

- **Business**

  As soon as you can, start getting an in-depth feel of how the corporate world works and what your particular industry is like. Find out the size of the market, who the main players are, what the current trends and the main issues are.

- **Your company**

  Find out, in broad terms, how the main departments in your company work and, more specifically, how your area or department works within that structure.

Know-how

By this, we mean think about the specific, practical skills you have, in areas such as computing, research or languages.

Cognitive ability

In the end, this comes down to being able to apply your knowledge in activities such as analysing situations, solving problems, making decisions, and planning and delegating work. It's the important skill of creative thinking.

People skills

We've already spoken of the importance of people and your relationships with them, so it's obvious they should have a place in your planning. The skills areas involved are equally obvious: you need to be able to empathise with others, communicate clearly and influence them. In other words, you need to be good at networking.

Attitude

This is probably even more important than your ability. Your attitudes to yourself, to work and to others are what conveys who you are to the outside world. So ask yourself these questions. Are you:

- **confident?**
  Do you believe in yourself?

- **positive?**
  Do you believe that everything's possible if you try?

- **proactive?**
  Can you motivate yourself and get started on something before you're asked?

- **resilient?**
  Do you think you have both emotional and intellectual strength?

- **flexible?**
  Do you have an open mind and are you receptive to new ideas and willing to change when necessary?

- **focused?**
  When you work, do you have a clear idea of the end product?

- **aware?**
  Even though you may just be part of it, can you see the big picture?

Marketing yourself

This sounds like a false, perhaps even cynical piece of advice. But it's true that, like products, people can have a 'brand image'. The problem is that it may not be the image you want because it's the result of how others see you and not necessarily what you're actually like. It's a difficult thing to control because the opinions of others define us and those 'others' can sometimes express strong views on the basis of very little information or interaction, or by misinterpreting something we've said or done. All of this suggests that, if you want to try to control how people see you, you'll have to learn to market yourself.

You as 'product'

First, try to find out if you already have a 'brand image' and, if so, what it is. Ask your boss at appraisal sessions, or just bring it up as you chat with colleagues. Once you've done that you'll know how you need to work on changing or strengthening it, so try to get a clear image of the characteristics you want people to associate you with. These are the qualities of you as product. If people aren't seeing them, you need to make some changes. We're not suggesting you try to be someone you're not. Base your image on qualities you know you have. You're not trying to fool people or being superficial, you're actively working to present yourself with recognisable, dependable characteristics. That's your 'brand image'.

brilliant tip

If you've no idea yet what your brand image is or might be, don't worry. As you progress, the way you need to be and how you need to present yourself will become clearer the more you see how others do it and the more certain you are of your own aims.

Your 'market'

It's no good having a great brand if nobody sees or 'buys' it, so work out which market you're selling to. It might be your boss, colleagues, peers, clients, some senior people in your company or any number of others. Each group may respond to the brand in a different way, so make sure you match it to whichever group you're with.

When you're with senior people in the company, make the most of the chance to impress. Don't waste their time but let them know what you're doing. If you feel the need to moan to them, resist it. They aren't interested in whiners; you need to be positive, upbeat and dynamic.

Your 'marketing strategy'

If you're still thinking this is all a bit artificial, you haven't grasped the importance of the process. The workplace is a competitive environment, so don't feel bad about marketing yourself. If you don't do it, no one else will. Just make sure you do it in a controlled, sensitive and definitely non-aggressive way. You can't be all things to all people, so keep your brand image consistent. You should be able to tell someone clearly and precisely what you're working on in just 30 seconds.

Giving the brand substance

Excellent advertising campaigns are sometimes so good that the product itself can't match the hype and turns out to be disappointing. Marketing yourself doesn't just mean boasting, there's got to be something solid, recognisable and true in the image you're projecting. It's relatively easy to identify the basic components of an effective self-image.

Competence

You've obviously got to be good at your job. Work hard to achieve this, never leave work unfinished and, if you make mistakes, admit them and learn from them. If you have a good grasp of the basics of what you do, whether it's technical or creative (or both), you can focus on things that matter and get results. Check your work thoroughly, deliver on time and, to lapse into a familiar piece of jargon, try to add value to the job, which basically boils down to trying to find better ways to do it.

Self-confidence

There's a fine line between self-assurance and arrogance; make sure you stay on the right side of it. If people start thinking of you as arrogant, it's a hard label to shake off. Make your body language positive in the way you walk and stand, think of what you need to say, and express yourself clearly and with confidence. But if you're not sure of something, ask about it; this'll help defuse any ideas that you're pompous. Give credit to others where it's due and, if you're praised, accept it graciously without embarrassment. Focus all the time on what you can do, not what you can't do.

An ability to empathise

It's a constant theme through the book but it's worth restating. Treat others in the way you'd like them to treat you. Make it easy for people to approach you and show them that you care.

Integrity

This shouldn't need saying but it's part of adding true substance to the image. Be totally trustworthy. Always tell the truth, although sometimes be prepared to wrap it up a little in order to be diplomatic and avoid hurting someone's feelings. Be loyal to your company, boss and colleagues both when you're with them and when they're not there and someone is talking about them.

brilliant tip

Don't join the rumour-mongers. Spreading rumours, betraying confidences or badmouthing colleagues and the company they work for always rebounds badly on the people who do it. It's unprofessional and earns them a bad reputation.

A positive approach

Whenever people meet or are interacting, it always helps to smile and, if it's appropriate, laugh. It's part of creating an aura of positivity, a feeling that things can be achieved. If you have that 'can-do' attitude and approach problems with solutions in mind, it'll give your brand a real boost.

Looking right

Maybe it shouldn't, but appearance does matter. This doesn't mean everyone should glide about the place like a supermodel, but it does mean you should think of the impression you're creating by the way you dress. It sends out a clear message about how you see yourself and how you expect to be treated. Think, too, of what your clients expect of you. Do they want you to look creative or reliable? The secret is to find a nice balance between conformity and individuality. If you're not sure what to wear, look at someone you respect and use them as a sort of guide. If in doubt, remember that it's safer to be too formal than not formal enough.

You don't have to spend a fortune, just try to look:

- **Smart**
  Don't wear jeans, tracksuits, big woolly jumpers or anything you'd wear if you were just lazing around at home. T-shirts or sweatshirts with slogans or statements are also out, and so-called 'humorous' ties, socks or cufflinks are rarely funny and may not carry the message you intend. A classic suit is fine. Stick to 'safe' colours and keep patterns and jewellery to a minimum.

- **Tidy**
  Don't carry handbags or briefcases that are scuffed, dirty or full of rubbish. The same applies to diaries; if they're bulging with extra bits of paper sticking out of them, they don't portray you as a busy individual with lots of appointments but as someone who can't keep things

organised. And a good pen creates a better impression than a cheap biro. Keep your glasses clean (and, given some of the fashions available nowadays, discreet).

● **Groomed**

This means keeping your hair and nails clean. Go easy on the gel or extravagant hairstyles and, if you wear nail varnish, keep it subtle. The same goes for make-up, perfumes and aftershaves. If they're fresh, clean and light it's OK but some are overpowering and they can trigger allergic reactions in some people.

 **brilliant** recap

● Points to consider when planning your career.

● Making a plan and putting it into practice.

● The main elements in personal development.

● Creating your brand image and marketing yourself.

CHAPTER 19

Office politics and other murky areas

At work, office politics and social events are inescapable. They can cause stress when people don't understand what's going on and suspect there are hidden messages and secret agendas behind seemingly normal contacts, but they can also benefit groups and individuals by motivating them and making it clear what does and doesn't contribute to the company's overall success. Here we'll look at how it all works and suggest ways of coping with and profiting from social events and political manoeuvrings.

There's nothing either good or bad ...

... at least that's what Shakespeare wrote, and the same could be said about office politics. So, you should get used to the fact that it's an inevitable part of company life. This is true not only of the workplace but of any large group of people. The reason it may seem more intense at work is that all employees have their own career plans and the various groups and departments have specific agendas, so alliances and competition are all part of the game.

Play the game

You often hear people asking who the main 'players' are in a particular commercial scenario, and the notion of business as a game is quite common. This doesn't mean that it's not serious and, even though the expression is often used to imply an unpleasant, negative context, it can be a positive force. If the process of influencing and persuading people is just aimed at promoting self-interest and for personal gain, especially at the expense of others, it's unethical and dirty. But it can just as well work positively to influence others to achieve goals that are for the good of the organisation as a whole and, as a consequence, everyone in it.

 **brilliant** tip

As we've seen, politics can be positive or negative. Don't subscribe to the negative aspects. If you get a reputation as a political animal, make sure you're firmly in the positive camp.

Be prepared to make it part of how you operate. You'll be depending on others to get your job done and, since they'll have their own personal agendas, playing politics will be part of how you interact. It's rare for anyone to stress the need to develop political skills in the workplace, and yet they're one of the most important attributes you'll need in liaising with people and making your own way upwards.

Survival skills

However politically aware you are (or aren't), you can still improve your political skills. Once you've experienced the different levels of political activities around you, you should try to develop the characteristics you'll need to join in and use them effectively yourself. The main ones can easily be identified. You need to be:

- **Informed ...**
  ... which means knowing where the power lies and how to get access to it, being aware of what's going on both in your own department and in the company as a whole.

- **Perceptive ...**

  ... in the way you note and try to understand the aspirations and motivations of other people so that you can anticipate how they may react in different situations.

- **Persuasive ...**

  ... which involves communicating well, in both speaking and writing, and learning to influence others. It'll help if you're honest with yourself about your own power and realistic about how much influence you have over your boss and colleagues.

- **Assertive ...**

  ... and ready to be strong-willed and stand up for your beliefs when it's necessary, because, if you don't do it, no one will do it for you.

- **Diplomatic ...**

  ... which may involve giving in to the demands of others if need be and trying not to offend anyone. (But note that it is possible to be both diplomatic and assertive.)

- **Flexible...**

  ... because at work and in every political situation change is inevitable. Friends can become enemies and vice versa, so you need to be able to adapt accordingly.

- **Wary ...**

  ... because people can take advantage of your openness and honesty. Assess others carefully before opening up to them and giving them your trust. Be particularly vigilant with those who feel threatened by you.

- **Principled ...**

  ... in your judgements. Trust your instincts because, if something you're doing or saying feels wrong or uncomfortable, it usually means that it is wrong. There may be short-term gains now and then in being dishonest or deceitful but it'll work against you in the long run.

The office party and other hurdles

There's a whole mythology about office parties but they're useful events so, even if you don't want to go, force yourself. You don't need to stay too long; just put in an appearance; show willing. Find out who'll be there and think about things you may want to talk about with them. It's a social occasion but that doesn't stop you having an informal chat about a work topic – just don't make it too long or too serious. And it's a good idea to eat something before you go; it wouldn't be too good for your image if you spent your time there stuffing yourself with food.

Circulate

The easy way out is to latch on to people you already know well, but you should use this chance to get to know others. Remember, it's all part of projecting your brand image, so smile and try to look as if you're enjoying yourself. If your boss is there, by all means have a chat with her, but don't monopolise her – she'll want to meet others too.

Wear a name badge if there are any and don't hesitate to introduce yourself to people you don't know. Try not to get into any heavy debates or discussions – keep the conversation light and avoid potentially dangerous topics. For example, don't get personal or be indiscreet. If you have secrets about others, keep them to yourself. Don't moan and complain about work, your boss or your colleagues. And make sure you don't ask about things that might make the people you're talking to feel uncomfortable. For example, if they don't want to drink or if they decide to leave early, don't ask why.

Be careful not to talk too much; give others a chance to say something. But if all they want to do is moan or just gossip, move away when you can. And, while you may think you're fascinating, don't assume that others will want to listen if all you're doing is talking about yourself.

 **brilliant** tip

People will be more likely to approach you if you're standing than if you're sitting. But resist the temptation to park yourself by the drinks or buffet table all evening.

Don't stop being professional

It's OK to be relaxed and informal but be careful not to over-step the mark when you're talking to senior management. Wear something appropriate and don't be too friendly or indulge in flirting. When it comes to drink, stick with what you know and be very careful to stay within your limits. The booze may be free but the consequences of over-indulgence could be very costly. If you do start to feel the effects, switch to water, and, if you think it could be a problem or if you feel ill, make your excuses and leave quietly.

brilliant tip

If you do something that you regret, don't pretend it didn't happen. Apologise sincerely as soon as you can but don't make a production number out of it. Move on and make sure you learn from the experience.

Office romances

It's not uncommon for two people who work together to be attracted to one another. This doesn't necessarily mean there's anything wrong with it but there's clearly a possibility that it might affect the way one or both of you work. So you need to think carefully about it and be aware of the impact it might have on how you do the job and how you relate to others around you.

Before you commit to it, make sure that it's more than just a brief infatuation. Give it a couple of weeks and, during that time, be very discreet so that tongues don't start wagging. Don't come to work together or leave at the same time; don't always have lunch together or hang around one another's desks. Then if, after giving it time, you think it is serious, make sure company policy doesn't discourage relationships between people in the same team or department. If they do, it might involve one of you moving to another part of the company. But if it is OK, don't suddenly make a big announcement; speak to your boss or head of department privately, then let people know about it as naturally as possible.

brilliant tip

Whatever type of relationship it is – brief or long-term – always be mature and discreet about it. Don't indulge in public displays of affection and don't, under any circumstances, have any sort of sexual interaction.

Be careful to make sure that it doesn't affect your work in any way. Think about how it may impact on your job and how you relate to your colleagues (especially if you're dating your boss). Don't spend all the time together and, if there are any work issues that involve your partner, be ultra careful in making sure that you treat them in the same way you treat others.

The office grapevine

This is a sort of informal network which has been around since long before the Internet, intranets and just about every other communications system. Information gets passed around, amended, exaggerated and either disappears or turns out to be informed and real. Anyone can be part of the grapevine but it tends to operate between people who get on well together.

In fact, it can be a useful source of inside information, so it's worth your while finding out who has the inside track on it and easing your way into their communication network if you can. You don't want to get too involved in it, but it's useful to know what rumours are doing the rounds. If what's being said about someone is negative, harmful or just plain wrong, though, let them know about it. Be careful how you do it. You don't want to get too involved or bring yourself trouble, but negativity of this sort can be corrosive and helps no one.

brilliant tip

If there's a really active grapevine, the possibility of having a truly private conversation is remote. People promise not to tell, but not all of them keep their word. Equally, if someone tells you something that they heard in confidence, you'll know you can't trust them, so don't reveal anything about yourself.

Use it with care

As we've said, many of the rumours that fly around are false, so think hard before you base anything you do on information that came through the grapevine. Gossip of all sorts is part of life generally, but, when it's spiteful or malicious, it helps no one and can hurt lots. Steer clear of such negativity and let people know you're not interested in hearing it.

brilliant tip

If someone's badmouthing a colleague who isn't there to defend himself, make it clear you don't want to hear it. It may mean you're left out of the claque, you could feel isolated but, in the long run, you'll be respected for it and trusted more.

brilliant recap

- How office politics work and how to use and/or survive them.
- The value of office parties and their potential dangers.
- The dos and don'ts of office relationships.
- How the grapevine works.

CHAPTER 20

The life/work balance

Your job's obviously an important part of your life and you take it seriously, but all too often people let its stresses and strains overcome the other parts of their lives – relationships, friends, family, hobbies, fun and just relaxation – and they're just as important. If you don't enjoy these important things, the tension, frustration and lack of fulfilment you feel can seep into everything you do, including the job itself, and you're in a vicious spiral. The secret is to keep all these elements in a healthy balance to get the most out of all of them and be a good person to be around. It's easy to say but maybe not so easy to do; nonetheless, it's worth working at it and enjoying life.

Working at keeping the balance right

You can start by making things simpler for yourself. Think of all the things you do and want to do, decide which are the important ones and focus on them. If some of the things you do are a source of stress or make your life more complicated, cut right back on them or get rid of them altogether. It may be hard at first but you'll soon feel the benefits.

Get yourself organised by making the most of facilities that are available to you. For example, set up direct debit accounts to pay all your bills; arrange a set time to do domestic chores. (If you can afford it, you can forget about this by hiring someone to do them for you for a couple of hours a week.) Letting house-work pile up can quickly make you feel you're not in control and, the longer you leave it, the worse it gets.

Meet with your boss and discuss your working style. Let him know you like the job and want to do it well but that you'll be even better at it if you can keep a balance between it and your life outside. Ask him how late he expects you to work and let him know you think it's reasonable to keep at least one day of the weekend (but preferably both Saturday and Sunday) free from work-related issues.

brilliant tip

Keeping this separation between home and the office is very important. Don't take work home with you unless it's something critical and there's a deadline to meet. Even then, it's better to do it at work and switch off from it when you go home.

Learn to say no. Naturally enough, you want to appear keen and willing but, if you say yes every time you're asked to do something, you're adding to your workload and the consequent pressures will keep building up. Don't agree to do something if you feel you don't have the emotional or physical energy, the time or perhaps even the brain power to cope with it easily.

Watch out for money troubles – they're a familiar source of anxiety and stress. Here, too, it's a question of balance. It's much easier to spend less than it is to earn more, so make sure you don't spend more than, or even as much as, you earn. If you can save some money, you'll always have control.

Look after yourself

If you're focusing intently on work, it's easy to forget to take care of yourself properly. Instead of eating sensibly, getting some exercise and having a good night's sleep, it's easier to grab a quick snack (probably of junk food), have no time for exercise and cut down on sleep time. You have to discipline yourself to follow a routine which makes sure your lifestyle is healthy. Work demands may sometimes creep in to disrupt the routine but keep it in mind and get back to it as soon as you can.

Food

Don't skip meals. Even if you're busy, stop and take a time out to eat. If you genuinely don't have time, instead of going out for lunch, ask someone to bring something back for you, but don't eat it while you're working. Stop and switch off, even if it's only briefly.

Sandwiches, crisps, chocolate and other convenience and processed foods are low in vitamins, nutrients and energy, so cut down on them. Instead, make sure you have some fresh fruit at least every other day. Reduce your intake of tea and coffee and drink plenty of water – 1½ litres a day is the recommended amount. And don't eat just before you go to bed – give yourself at least two hours to digest the meal.

brilliant tip

Every evening, when you get home, go for a five-minute walk. It'll slow you down, clear your mind, stretch your legs and get some clean air into your lungs. It'll also help you to sleep.

Relaxation

Exercise is important and you should try to get a minimum of 30 minutes of cardiovascular exercise at least three times a week. Take the stairs rather than use the lift and walk rather than drive or take a taxi. It's just as important, though, to slow everything down and relax. If you're stressed, try yoga or one of the other meditation techniques; do something you enjoy that relaxes you and takes your mind off other things. And try to get at least seven hours of sleep every night. It also helps if you get a pattern of going to bed and waking up at the same time every day, even at weekends.

Managing stress

Feeling stressed sometimes is normal – the real issue is how strong and how frequent the feelings are and how you react to them. And, this depends entirely on you because stress is your personal response to pressure. It may be caused by something outside yourself – a colleague's unreasonableness, your workload, domestic issues – but, equally, it can be generated from inside you. We all know how it can affect a person's mental and physical well-being so it's something we should confront, not ignore.

Your stress personality

We all get stressed now and then but some people seem to be less prone to it than others. If you're a worrier, it's hard to just switch it off, but it can help to understand what sort of stress personality you have.

 **examples**

- **Brian** has the ostrich approach. He prefers not to believe that anything's wrong. Despite all the evidence to the contrary, he always hopes that the problem will go away. Eventually, though, it's so pressing that he has to acknowledge it, by which time it's become serious and the stress it causes is much greater. He needs to be more honest with himself, more aware of how he's feeling and responding to situations and events. Keeping a diary would help him to see the sorts of things that trigger stress and the patterns of his own feelings as they develop. It would help, too, if he could talk things over with someone. In fact, it might be a good idea to see a counsellor.

- **Beth** certainly feels stressed at times but she masks it and, even in a crisis, always presents the appearance of being cool and organised. The problem here is that her colleagues don't realise that she's churning inside and so they can unknowingly add to the stress by making demands on her. She really needs to learn to say no so that she can concentrate on handling the stress rather than adding to it.

- Everyone knows when **Kate**'s under pressure – she gets irritable, quick-tempered and snaps their heads off when they ask even innocent questions. She needs to learn some simple relaxation techniques. She also needs to be kinder to herself and accept that she doesn't have to be perfect all of the time.

- **Ben** is Kate multiplied by several. He's twitchy, overly sensitive and, when things get on top of him (as they frequently do), he just blows his top. For his own sake, as well as that of those around him, he needs to bring a little more calm into his life. It's not rocket science; the simple techniques of doing some deep breathing or counting to ten are a start. It would also help if he cut down drastically on his intake of stimulants such as caffeine, chocolate, tea, cola and sugar.

Keep things in perspective

At the beginning of the previous chapter, we quoted a line from Shakespeare's *Hamlet*:

> There's nothing either good or bad
> But thinking makes it so.

And that's exactly how stress works. If you're a worrier, you'll see not just the negatives of the situation itself but project them into the future and feel stressed about their possible consequences, too. In other words, you're upsetting yourself not only about things that haven't yet happened but also about other things that might happen if they do. It's totally illogical. But, of course, logic doesn't play a very big role where anxiety is concerned.

If that's the way you operate, you should try hard to be realistic in how you're perceiving the situation that's causing the stress. Is it really as bad as you think? Compare it with other possibilities, other situations. Is it really important enough to be worth getting stressed about? And if that doesn't work, balance it by thinking about all the positives in your life. You can even make a list of them so that you have the evidence of them there in front of you.

Don't obsess about a possible future event. It may never happen, so deal with each day as it comes. Think about where you'll be in a few months, a year. Will whatever it is that's worrying you now still be a factor? Will you even remember it happened at all?

Get away from it

Whatever the source of the worry, make yourself escape from it, mentally, physically or both. Stop work and read a magazine or a newspaper for a while; go for a walk, preferably in a park. If you feel you really need to let off steam, do some strenuous exercise and get it all out of your system. And if you can't leave the office, just get away from your desk, find somewhere quiet and meditate for five minutes. Just empty your mind; make yourself stop thinking.

brilliant tip

Close your eyes and focus on your breathing. Then systematically make yourself relax. Start by concentrating on your toes and work your way up to your head, relaxing each muscle one by one. Let yourself sink into the relaxation.

One of the causes and the effects of stress is focusing on negatives, so stop thinking of how bad things are and concentrate on what you can do and get on with it. Be positive. You can always do something, no matter how awful things seem. Tidy your desk, clear your clutter, write a list of everything you need to do – it doesn't matter what it is, if you're doing something it'll help you to feel you're in control. Just get a picture in your mind of everything working out the way you want it to. And don't hesitate to ask someone for help; their response to it may make you see the problem differently.

brilliant tip

Accept the fact that you won't always feel terrific or do the right thing. Don't punish yourself for not being perfect. In fact, do the opposite: give yourself a treat. Make a list of all the things that make you feel good – a massage, a hot bath, funny movies, whatever – and, when you're not feeling great, pick one or two from the list and indulge yourself. Don't underestimate the value of laughter and the pleasure principle.

Beat stress before it arrives

We spoke of stress personalities. Try to work out what triggers your stress; if you can identify and understand the signs, you'll be better placed to anticipate them and do something to manage how you're feeling. The important thing to remember is that you can't change anyone else, but you can change yourself. If it's your boss or a colleague who's doing something that irritates you or gets you worked up, the only way of dealing with it is by changing how you react to them. That's an important message: quite often it's not the stress itself that's the problem, but how you respond to it.

Travel and stress

More and more jobs today involve travelling abroad. It sometimes sounds glamorous but usually isn't. The process of getting from A to B can be tedious and try your patience. And, of course, it has lots of potential for creating stress. If you're aware of this and prepare properly, you can minimise the chances of getting too upset.

Before you leave

When it comes to booking, if you don't particularly like flying, try to get a seat that's over the wing – that's the most stable part of the aircraft. If legroom's important, you need to ask to sit either in the front row or in the one next to the emergency exit.

On long-haul flights, especially to different time-zones, choose your seat to suit how you want the flight to go. If you intend to sleep on the plane, book a flight that'll get you to your destination in the morning and a window seat to make sure you're not disturbed by neighbours wanting to get past you. On the other hand, if you find it difficult to sleep while flying, book a flight that'll get you there in the evening and an aisle seat so that you can move about.

Make a list of the things you'll need and use it to confirm that you've packed all the essentials. This will include passport, money, tickets, credit cards and all the information you need about your trip. As well as your itinerary and directions to your destination when you land, make sure you have the names and numbers of everyone you'll be meeting while you're there.

brilliant tip

The personal stuff is up to you but you'll obviously want toothbrush, shaving kit, make-up, any regular medication you need and an extra change of clothes in case you have to stay longer than you'd planned.

Book a cab with a reliable company to make sure you get to the airport in plenty of time. In fact, you should work out when you should leave, then add a comfort zone to it. Start tidying up at work earlier than you think you need to.

Wear what you feel most comfortable in and, if you can, just take carry-on luggage, which means travelling as light as you can.

During the flight

As soon as you get on the plane, switch to the time zone you're travelling to. When you're in the air, avoid caffeine and alcohol – they'll dehydrate you. Drink lots of water instead. Don't eat too much. In fact, it's better to eat before you leave, if you can. Don't stay seated for the whole flight; move about now and then, and while you are sitting, do the exercises you'll find in the in-flight magazine. When you arrive, go for a brisk walk – but not if it's the dead of night.

brilliant tip

Make your stay as enjoyable and as normal as you can. Unwind after work, go to the gym, the cinema, socialise with friends or colleagues for dinner. Make the working part worthwhile but also relax and enjoy it.

Managing your time

Deadlines, several tasks piling up and needing to be done at the same time, and the whole 'not-enough-time-in-the-day' feeling all create and contribute to stress. If you get yourself, and especially your timetable, properly organised, you can reduce their impact. Good time management helps you to achieve the vital balance between the various tasks your job involves and also the different elements of your home life.

As with everything else, there isn't a 'one size fits all' solution. You need to understand your own preferences in terms of when you're best at thinking and when you're best at putting thoughts into action. We all have times of the day when we feel at our most productive, so work this out for yourself and schedule your activities to make the most of that time. It may be that, at the end of the day, you're tired and not at your best, so that's the time for semi-automatic activities such as tidying your desk or arranging files.

Forward planning and prioritisation

It's important to be honest and realistic about what you can achieve. Draw up a plan of all the various things you need to do at the beginning of the week and fit them into slots which are best suited to the sorts of demands they'll be making on you. Don't cram them all together; be flexible and try to leave gaps everywhere in case activities over-run or the unexpected happens (which it usually does).

 **tip**

Every evening before you leave work, try writing a 'To Do' list for the following day. Also, at the end of the week, list all the things you have to do or want to achieve in the following week.

When you're drawing up these lists, don't give everything equal status – decide which things are important and urgent and which are trivial. This lets you group them into obvious categories such as 'Must do', 'Should do' or 'Would be nice to do if there's time'. You can now prioritise them and do the essential things first and leave the 'nice to do' stuff until you've finished the rest. Resist the temptation to do little jobs just to get them out of the way; fit everything into the place that your priorities dictate. But don't forget to include breaks; stopping for lunch – even if it's just a quick snack – is important. And don't be surprised to find that everything seems to take longer than you expect it will.

Put the plans into action

Don't make this list creation a displacement activity. It's all too easy to put things off and convince yourself you're doing something when all you're doing is refining your schedules. Make a start. The longer you put something off, the harder it is to get going on it and the more anxiety you start building up about getting it done. It's there, it needs doing, so do it. Make a habit of starting a task as soon as you get it and try to finish it ahead of time.

If you don't think you're achieving much with a particular activity, delegate it and move to something more productive. Save all the trivial tasks, such as answering emails and making phone calls, and group them all together to do at a time when you're not feeling very energetic.

When you work, always be aware of where you're heading and what you're trying to achieve. Ask yourself whether what you're doing at a particular point is the best use of your time. And force yourself to say 'no' to unreasonable requests.

brilliant tip

If you can arrange it so that you start work early, even if only by 20 minutes or half an hour, you can get well ahead of schedule and stay there throughout the day.

When it comes to paperwork, you should apply the same principle of dealing with it as soon as you receive it. If it's better dealt with by someone else, pass it to them at once with a note saying why you're doing so – that's not dodging your responsibility; it's being efficient. If it's something you need to act on, either do so at once or add a note to your list to schedule it for the earliest opportunity. If you don't know what to do with something, don't file it; either find out what it's about or bin it.

Keep your files organised in ways that make it easy for you to access what you want quickly and get rid of anything you don't need. Once a month, it's worth devoting 15 minutes or so to going through the materials you have and eliminating excess.

Time is precious. Don't waste it.

brilliant recap

- The importance of getting the right balance between work and home life.
- Staying healthy, eating well and learning to relax.
- The causes of stress and some ways of defusing anxieties.
- Taking the stress out of travel.
- The essentials of time management, planning and implementing the plans.

Conclusion: be yourself

We're all different things to different people. We adapt our manners, way of speaking, appearance and overall behaviour to suit the particular role we're playing at any one time. The angry, red-faced individual at the football match swearing at the referee, the father reading his child a bedtime story, the dutiful son sending his mum a card for Mother's Day, the driver fuming at the wheel on the brink of road rage, the manager gently talking one of his workers through a crisis – they're all the same person. We slip in and out of all our roles without thinking.

To complicate it still further, at the same time another set of roles is being imposed on us by other people. They may see our modesty as hypocrisy, our confidence as arrogance, our unwillingness to jump to conclusions as weakness. And we're doing exactly the same thing with them. So, the primary workplace skill in the end is to be sure of who you are, be prepared for others not always to agree with that version of you, and to be honest and consistent in the way you treat them.

Despite the fact that we've been stressing the need to project a specific image, to think – and, yes, to calculate – before you make decisions or commit to something, we don't want to suggest that the workplace is some sort of stage where you put on another, artificial personality. On the contrary, the more you can be yourself and convey that image to others, the more likely you are to succeed.

Of course, you can become a caricature if you choose, and tell your customers that, 'Our mission statement includes a holistic determination to share our vision, achieve the appropriate state of synergy with our clients, stay ahead of the curve with some blue sky thinking and deliver satisfactory levels of forecast performance metrics. These are the desired deliverables, so our firm commitment is to leverage feedback informationwise.'

Alternatively, you can choose to be the more relaxed version of the same person and tell your team, 'OK guys, we want to push the envelope, think outside the box but stay on the same page and hit the ground running. If we're singing from the same hymn sheet, we'll be able to walk the walk, talk the talk AND walk the talk. That'll tick all the boxes and we'll be in a win-win situation. So let's run it up the flagpole and see who salutes it.'

But be warned: if these are the sorts of path you take, there aren't many who'll follow you down them. Yes, you'll hear – and be obliged to use – jargon and strange acronyms, but the more you assume them to have more power than your normal way of speaking or writing, the further you'll disappear into a stifling anonymity or, worse, a joke.

You're not going to please all of the people all of the time, but, if you play by the rules and treat others the way you want them to treat you, you'll earn their respect and trust. Above all, be yourself. Sometimes this may mean admitting you're wrong or that you've made a mistake, and sometimes it'll mean being assertive and arguing your corner. In the end, the real job satisfaction is knowing that you, and the other real people around you, haven't just spent the required number of hours at work – you've made a difference.

Index

Be Brilliant at University

Get started on your graduate career

Brilliant Graduate Career Handbook **gives you the help and information you need to get started on your graduate career – what's out there, how to make sense of it, and how to make good choices.**

Brilliant Outcomes:

✓ Understand the labour market and how to navigate it

✓ Begin to decide what to do with your degree once you have graduated

✓ Learn how to make the best use of opportunities around to develop your skills and experience for the future

Available from **www.pearson-books.com** and all good bookshops